GOING FERAL
Field Notes on
Wonder & Wanderlust

by Heather Durham

TRAIL TO TABLE PRESS
Eastsound, Washington
An imprint of Wandering Aengus Press

Library of Congress Cataloguing-in-Publication Data available.

ISBN: 978-0-578-44281-5

Cover Image © Tyler Doyle
Author Photo by Jared Archbold

Some of the essays in this volume were previously published in earlier versions by the following publications:
"Destiny Manifested" first published in *Cirque Literary Journal*, 7.1.
"Earth to Earth" first published in *Blue Lyra Review*, 5.3.
"Feral" first published in *Soundings Review*, Summer 2016.
"Hand Wing" first published in *Tahoma Literary Review*, Issue 6, Vol. 3.1.
"Prey" first published in *Animal Literary Magazine*, Aug. 1, 2018.
"Blood and Ink" first published in *Bacopa Literary Review*, Volume 7, 2016.

Project editors: Julie Riddle and Jill McCabe Johnson
Design: Jill McCabe Johnson

Trail to Table Press is an imprint of Wandering Aengus Press.
PO Box 334 Eastsound, WA 98245.
www.trailtotable.net

Printed in the United States of America.

Dialogue and events are presented to the best of the author's ability, representing people as accurately as possible. To protect their privacy, the names and identifying characteristics of some of the individuals mentioned in this book have been changed.

FIRST EDITION

Table of Contents

Part 1: Imprints

Glint of Sun

I'm dreading the solo. Three days alone on an island? No thank you. I understand it's part of the whole Outward Bound philosophy, "to serve, to strive, and not to yield," that being alone with little food and barely any gear is supposed to make me stronger, to teach me something. Right, like being sent to my room as a kid was supposed to teach me something. Maybe I could just sleep for three days.

We've already done plenty of striving in this first part of our month-long trip, the sailing portion. Ten students new to sailing and two instructors on a thirty-foot sailboat attempting to navigate the rocky coast of Maine in May, awesome. The wind never stops out here, which I guess is good for sailing but it's wicked cold, bitter cold, and there's no coming in from it. My hands and face are the only parts exposed but they are already red and cracking, not sure from the cold or the wind or the sun. Probably all of it.

It's 2:30 in the morning and I'm on night watch, making

sure the boat stays anchored and we don't drift off to sea or back toward the rocky shore. I'm supposed to wake everyone up at 3 a.m. to get moving before the tides turn so we can reach Hurricane Island outpost by midday. I'm in the bow, using my headlamp to see my journal because it's dark as a dungeon out here, even under all those stars. The others are sleeping, head to toe on the oars laid out between masts, which isn't as uncomfortable as you'd think. Maybe we're just so tired we don't notice.

We started sailing from headquarters on the mainland and have been busting our butts to make it through Penobscot Bay in six days, a zig-zagging sixty miles to Hurricane Island, where we will spend one night together on land before they dump us off on our own islands for three days, pick us up and take us back to the island basecamp to spend a few days before driving north for the canoeing portion of the trip.

In addition to the cold and the hard work of navigating the winds – we all have rope burns – we hardly get any sleep. A long night is 11 p.m. to 5 a.m., but so far that was only once, and otherwise we've had to be bound by the wind and tides. As if that wasn't enough, each day they find some land where we anchor, hop off, and run for five miles and then jump in the ocean. The ocean! In May! It's hard to breathe jumping into liquid ice – the instructors are always right there, ready to pull you out in case you can't catch your breath because the cold sort of collapses your lungs, or it feels that way. But when you manage to get out that's the warmest you feel all day, and for two minutes or so you don't even need all your layers. Until the wind blows away the warm and you're shivering again.

Everything hurts. My arms from pulling on ropes and my legs from running and my throat from the wind plus dehydration and my head from the sun on the water. But you know what? I'm happy. This is one of the hardest things I've ever done but I'm having a great time! At least I think I am. I actually haven't had much time to think about it. It helps that we're all in this together.

I just met these people but I'm going to miss them over the solo. Especially Sara, who's nineteen, from Maine, and even though she's homesick, loves to sing. She knows all the words to "American Pie," which comes in handy when you're trying to distract yourself from seasickness on yet another hazy afternoon on choppy water. And twenty-five-year-old Tony from Rochester, New York, who's your basic teddy-bear jock – I think he's actually a gym coach – tells the best jokes. Emily from Kentucky is only eighteen, and is quiet but very sweet and encourages everyone. I'll even miss Rich, a big guy in his thirties who is the only one slower than I am on our morning runs. He has a funny word for everything and always states the obvious, but that isn't as annoying as you'd think.

John and Terri are our leaders. John is mid-thirties, looks like Robin Williams, is a strong leader and very supportive. Terri is late twenties, mom-like, and enunciates every word, sort of like she's from overseas.

Who am I? I am twenty-one and maybe a little judgmental on the inside, but on the outside, I do my best to be agreeable and helpful, to never complain and not get in the way. I'm not funny or skilled in anything we're doing, but I try hard, cheer the others on, and always keep smiling. I hope they like me.

My watch is almost up. Time to go hang off the side of the boat and pee before I have to wake everyone up. That part is sort of fun, much more so than pooping in a bucket in front of everyone.

~

I'm alone now. On an island. Totally and completely alone. Marooned! For three days. Help?

I actually teared up when the motorboat sped away. I stood

there on the bare granite, holding my duffle bag, and I waved until I couldn't see them anymore, like a little kid left by the side of the road as her family drove away. I'm such a big baby.

But I had work to do before darkness, so I got busy. Busy is good. The first thing I did was to try to make myself a home. I found a good level spot right away, up in the trees far above the high tide line. All they gave us was a tarp and some string, but I tried my best to make a sort of tent. It took a long time because I wanted to get it right, to secure the middle of one edge of the tarp to some branches so the wind wouldn't take it and to angle it so the coming rain won't puddle back in on me. I found an extra piece of string left on one of the trees here, probably from another solo, and that made me feel less alone. For a minute. I found a weathered board that must have washed up and used it to anchor one side of the tarp but on the inside, so I have a shelf. I used rocks to weigh down the other side. After lots of scurrying, rearranging and fussing and fixing, it actually looks like a tent! I laid out my sleeping bag inside and will use my duffle bag of extra clothes as a pillow.

So. Now what? It's still early, only 7 p.m.. Which I know because I smuggled in my watch because I couldn't imagine trying to make it three days without knowing what time it is. It's 7 p.m. on Thursday. I'm alone in this wilderness until Sunday. What do I do now?

A better question would have been: who am I now? When nobody else was around, stripped of human relationships and busywork, when the external noise stopped and the inner quiet finally arrived, who were you?

All those words in my journal, babbling about other people and activities and whining about discomfort; who was I beneath that? Where was I?

I don't know if I can handle this. It's too quiet. And the mosquitoes are starting to come out. And it's starting to drizzle.

I'm going to bed.

~

You know what? It's really pretty here. This morning the sun is shining and the air is still and my clearing in the spruce trees overlooking the ocean is lovely. And I'm actually warm! I don't remember being warm this whole trip. I must be on the protected side of the island. My island.

I've just taken off my fleece jacket and am down to only my T-shirt and nylon pants. I grabbed a pile of smelly clothes from my duffle bag – underwear, long underwear, and my other t-shirts – and walked carefully down the sloping, barnacled granite to dip them in the salt water. They are all laid out next to me on the rocks, drying in the sun.

And now, the most exciting part of my day! I will eat one third of the bread they gave me. Three days and three pieces of food. One hunk of bread, one apple, one 2x2x2-inch block of cheese. Therefore, logically, I will eat a third of each on each day. Bread in the morning, apple midday, cheese in early evening.

Bread, oh bread! Caramel-colored honey whole wheat, fresh from the Hurricane Island kitchen where the white-haired ponytailed tie-dye-wearing old hippie gave us a lecture on eating real food, though I've heard it all before from my hippie parents and their health food co-ops, with their homemade granola, all-natural no-sugar peanut butter, and their wheat germ sprinkled on everything. I could do without the wheat germ, but real bread, yes! So delicious, almost sweet, the miracle of bread! I will eat every crumb. Sorry chipmunk squeaking at me from the forest. I see you, and you will get none of my bread. I will bury the rest of it with my other provisions deep in my duffle bag and close it tight.

Chipmunk! I guess it's just you and me. No large mammals, they told us; these islands are too small. That's a relief, anyway.

It's going to be hard enough to spend three days alone here without worrying about being eaten by bears.

Who else was there? Who else called that island home? What other small mammals – red squirrels perhaps, shrews, or mice? What about salamanders or frogs, deep in the forest where the rain puddles into vernal pools? Snakes, slithering out of the cool forest to sun themselves on the rocks? Birds! Surely you heard some birds in Maine in May? How could you not have noticed ANY birds?

The coast of Maine is full of these little deserted islands, ringed with naked granite with a spruce tree center. We learned they are summits of an ancient mountain range, poking out of the Atlantic like icebergs and equally barren. Guess I should go see how big this rock is. Nothing else to do.

~

Rounding the first corner, I spotted Rich over on his island. We both jumped up and down and waved like crazy, then sat watching each other for a while. It hasn't even been twenty-four hours yet! Continuing on, I soon realized that my island is not as small as I originally thought, and more oblong than round. Remnants from other Outward Bound soloists appeared among the pebbles and spruce cones – strange little monuments, geometric designs, and purposeful collections here and there. I am an anthropologist discovering vanished cities of one.

And those who came before? Post-colonial farming and logging operations? Granite quarries? Pre-colonial Abenaki or other tribal fishing camps? How might the landscape have looked one hundred years ago? How does it continue to change? Are all modern twenty-one-year-olds so insular as to not even consider that stuff?

Looking out across the water from the far side of my island I saw a red speck that I think was Emily. I wonder how the others are doing.

The winds picked up on that side and I was quickly chilled in my cotton T-shirt and thin pants, so I had to keep moving. I started to get nervous as the sun moved high in the sky and the island seemed to go on forever, doubting that I would see my happy tent again. Due to steep cliffs I had to stray into the dense forest a good deal, scratching my legs and straining my eyes to hold onto my sense of direction. After a couple hours, though, I found my way home.

How quickly a sense of home is created – partly from the few essentials there, but mainly from familiarity. Back to my blue tarp and red sleeping bag and driftwood board holding comb, journal, and pen, and blue flag hung by the cliff to tell passers-by that I am okay *(and chipmunks and spruce trees and birds and bugs and lichens and granite and a living landscape that I was getting to know as it was getting to know me, whether or not I realized that)*. John and Terri will drive by in the early afternoon; my job is to wave if all is well. So far, it is. Time to eat a third of apple.

Now there are two chipmunks, checking on me to see if I'm foolish enough to leave any food out. Not a chance. Mine.

A lobster fisherman just rode by, checking his traps. We waved at each other. That was fun.

I just did some stretching and some sit-ups and am now sitting in the sun in a place where the rock looks scooped out, a natural lounge chair. It's a little pokey because it's granite but with my towel laid out it's not so bad.

I don't know what to do now. What do I do now? I better figure something out or these three days will last forever. At least it's sunny.

It was sunny. Got that. What else? How many colors did you see in the ocean? What did the breeze sound like in the spruce trees, or rippling on the water? Could you smell the rafts of kelp, or the spruce pitch leaking from the wound in the closest tree? How about the dry spongy forest floor and understory thick with still unripe wild blueberries, highbush cranberry, and saskatoon that you won't get to know by name for several more years? How many different warblers sang from the treetops? What insects were they eating? From where did that damselfly hatch? Did you see any whales, porpoises, seals, or other marine mammals? How could you possibly feel alone surrounded by so many other lives? When will you learn to extend your awareness and desire for connection beyond your human peers?

They came to check on me at 2 p.m. There were four or five of them, probably other staff from the island. We waved to each other, and it made me so happy. I felt less alone for a few minutes, but now I'm alone again. Lonely.

This is harder than I thought it would be. I'm fighting that old empty feeling in the pit of my stomach that I only get when I'm by myself. I keep telling myself that I'm happy and that life is wonderful and it could be so much worse. After this trip I'm going back to work at Camp Takodah, then heading into senior year at UVA. I should appreciate this time, and I do, in theory. But I'm not as comfortable as I should be. I keep staring into space, thoughts wandering, then get annoyed with myself for doing nothing. For wasting my life minute by minute. At least I'm not angry here, not crazy like I get at home. Just so… lonely.

I want my friends. I want someone to hold, and to hold me. I want to fall in love again. I want it so much. Then this empty feeling will go away, even when I'm by myself.

No, it won't. You can't fill the emptiness with other people. Maybe that works for some people, but not for you. You will try, and you will fail. Over and over again. Each time you fail, the emptiness will swell. But it will go away, once you fill it with something else.

It's getting dark, and I'm still scared of the dark, so I better get in bed.

~

It's Saturday. I woke up at 8, which means I got twelve hours of sleep, but I didn't think I could get up. I felt so weak that I thought – that's it, up goes the red flag. But after slowly and shakily shedding a layer of clothing, drinking five cups of water and relaxing by the ocean in the sunshine, I feel ninety percent better. Still a little weak, but that's to be expected. Not to yield, right? Fine.

A voice just yelled "Hey!" and I looked directly across from my shelter and saw someone waving from yet another island. I can't tell who it is, a girl I think, but I don't much care. Right now I'll take anyone. I hadn't seen her before now, so maybe she is just walking around her island like I did yesterday.

I'm in better spirits than last night and thankful for another beautiful morning. Not a cloud in the sky, wind quiet, and ocean bluer than ever. And the bread did me good.

I made a present for someone, not sure who, and not sure what it is. Just some whittled sticks, some rope and string, some seaweed, a feather. *That's a start. What else might you have made? How else might you have reached out and touched the landscape, let it touch you, started seeing the natural world as more than just a static backdrop for your human life?*

I'm eagerly awaiting my check-up. I'm going to wave them in and get more water. I keep hearing fishing boats and thinking it's them. I hope they come soon.

I probably shouldn't be out in the sun so much but it makes me warm and happy. Mostly I just watch the water, the little rivulets in the wind, but I also just saw twenty-four ducks with many more ducklings. They were cute. I wish they stayed around longer. *Yes, good. See? More than just you out there.*

~

Yay, they came by at 1:30, earlier than yesterday. I got more water and got to say hi to Terri. I told her I was okay. I feel better now. I'm going to go walking.

~

I ended up walking the whole island again, this time in forty-five minutes. The tide was low so I could stay on the rocks on the periphery instead of angling inland. I must have gone way off course last time, walked in circles. I keep expecting the island to be round, only to find it's a sort of asymmetrical star with many inlets and outlets. I saw Rich on the way and we yelled some small talk. Aside from that, the only other news is that I'm developing two new blisters on my pinky toes.

Really? Blisters? That's all you got?

At least the walk passed some time. I found some beach peas – one of the wild edibles we learned about – and they were okay though kind of bitter, but they didn't seem to help my hunger at all. I just ate another third of my apple. I'd kill for a candy bar! Health food be damned – I want some Cool Ranch Doritos and a pint of Ben & Jerry's. *Yeah, that hasn't changed.*

I'm going to rest now. I'm glad the sun is still out. Late afternoon is the hardest part. Only one more day. One more lonely day.

~

That cheese just did not sit well in my stomach. Despite my hunger I could not bring myself to finish it, so I ended up throwing the rest into the forest. It's your lucky day, chipmunks! Hope you like mozzarella.

Why didn't you wait around to watch? Did they even eat

your smelly old cheese? What was their usual food? Were the two chipmunks rivals or a mated pair? Were they feeding a family, maybe hidden nearby? When had they stopped squeaking alarms at you, anyway?

Watching them could have been interesting. Watching them could have begun to satisfy a hunger you weren't even aware you had. Watching, wondering, and really seeing them could have started to awaken a voice and a consciousness that would mean the end of the word called loneliness. Because maybe you were never actually lonely for other people. All along, maybe you were lonely for the earth.

I'm looking forward to canoeing. We get to sleep on land every night. Thus far we've eaten, slept, and breathed ocean. We sailed on it, slept on the boat on it, swam in it, and I am now surrounded by it. I've always loved the ocean, but I am starting to feel saturated. Too much blue, too much flat dead water stretching on forever; it may as well be a desert. Too much water; not enough earth. Like the pit in my stomach right now. I think I'll turn in early tonight. Hopefully I'll sleep all night and into tomorrow. I know I'm wasting time, but I don't know what else to do.

~

It's finally Sunday! I got up at 7 am, jolted by a fog horn somewhere after an already choppy night's sleep. I first woke up at 1 to go to the bathroom and then a mosquito hounded me for an hour or so. I was also up at 4 and again at 6. But that's okay, because now I can justify a nap before I leave.

I ate the rest of my bread early today to give me strength to pack up. It took me a while to pack and put my tarp away, to leave no trace that I've been here. I left about the same amount of string as I'd found here. I changed my clothes and combed my hair into a fresh ponytail and feel much better. The chipmunks have been very active this morning; I think they know something is up.

Of course they did. And the birds you didn't notice. And, you will one day believe, the landscape itself. How did that little island see you? Like a tiresome little mosquito? A chipmunk, maybe. A naïve juvenile chipmunk. All chatter, no substance.

Despite your chatter, something of that island got into you anyway, didn't it? Something in the glint of sun on the water, in the waves licking the granite, in the wind in the trees, and in the underlying silences and spaciousness you couldn't fill with other people. You couldn't have put words to it, would not even begin to recognize it until much later, but this something sparked on a little island off the rocky coast of Maine would grow from a twinge to a hunger to a need you would spend years, a decade, a lifetime pursuing.

Now I'm sitting in my comfy rock spot, watching the water in case they come to get me early. I've heard some far-off motorboats but so far have only seen a sailboat and some kayakers. Only a few more hours, I hope. I can't believe I've been here three days! Sometimes it seems like more, sometimes less, but definitely not three days. I wish I'd made better use of my time here. I wish something interesting had happened. Or that I'd figured something out. I wish there weren't so many motorboats out right now.

I dozed until the sound of a motor made me jump again, but this boat was for me. Finally, rescued. Finally, people, companionship. I'm never going to spend so much time alone, ever again.

Terri said I look different, something about my eyes being clearer. I feel the same, but everything else seems changed. I went off and did nothing for three days and now the motorboat is faster, people are louder, and everything feels too close, crowding me. It is nice to see everyone, but...

I can't believe I'm saying this, but I'm actually dreading spending the next few days with all those people, all that noise at basecamp. Don't get me wrong; it's not that I want to go back to my island.

Do I?

I wonder how the chipmunks are doing.

Igneous Erratic

My eyes were open, but I couldn't see. Or rather, all I could see was a rosy glow through the folded bandana wrapped around my eyes, over the tops of my ears, and knotted under my ponytail. When the light dimmed suddenly, I knew we'd left the sunny meadow and were heading into the forest. I closed my eyes and let the haze go black.

Leda's arm linked through mine led me gently onward, her unruly curls tickling my shoulder above my scoop-neck T-shirt. I could hear a change in our steps and felt through my boots that we'd crossed the gravel road and stepped onto the soft dirt and pine needle path.

I was not scared. By twenty-two, I'd already trust-walked my way through acres of forest at my nearby summer camp. The fourteen others with us on that southern New Hampshire campus, leading or being led, silent ahead or still crunching gravel behind, were all adults. Staff in training at the Sargent Center for Outdoor

Education. This was just one activity in a three-ring binder full of experiential lessons we would be leading for visiting school children when we became the teachers, next week.

"Stop," Leda whispered, and I obeyed.

"There's a big rock in front of you. Feel it?"

I toed my boot forward until it thunked the rock, then extended a hand. Fingers probed in and out of crevices, alternately smooth and rough, sharp and rounded. We'd reviewed local geology the day before, and this felt like...granite? A colorful picture projected in my mind—flecks of pink feldspar, glassy black mica, and shining white quartz crystals. Igneous rock, born of fire.

Both hands reached out then, following the shape of the boulder. It was big. Taller than I could reach up and wider than I could stretch around. Following it to the ground, I poked my fingers into the soil under the rock and decided that it was not rising up from underground; it was not part of the bedrock. Just a big old rock plunked in the middle of the forest.

Where did it come from? When the last glacial ice retreated just over 10,000 years ago, New England was redecorated. Mammoth boulders froze and flowed with the ice then were left willy-nilly when the ice melted. This 'glacial erratic' was comfortably cool now, concealing the fire of its origins and the ice of its journey.

I gave the boulder a friendly farewell pat, found Leda's arm and let her lead me on. We crunched over sticks and a few of late summer's early fallen leaves, off the trail now and bushwhacking through the dry woods. I brushed spider webs from my face and stepped up when she said step up, ducked when she said duck. We scrambled over a low stone wall, a remnant of pioneer days when the forest was cleared and farmers' sheep roamed this landscape.

I was no 'child left inside.' I was not one of the ones we learned about who spent their days playing computer games and watching TV, who were scared of squirrels and uncomfortable walking on uneven ground instead of sidewalks. I'd slogged through swamps in Massachusetts. Romped through muddy cornfields and climbed apple trees in Connecticut. I cannonballed in lakes and strayed off-trail among poison ivy vines and prickly juniper thickets in New Hampshire, and backpacked through moose- and mosquito-infested wetlands in the North Maine Woods. Though this was my first real job out of college, this rustic outdoor school felt a lot like summer camp and I was perfectly at home. So why, in that first two weeks of outdoor school, did I feel I was discovering the natural world for the first time?

"Here. Do you know this tree?"

Did I? I reached out and touched smooth flat needles. I grasped and shook a branch as if shaking a hand. In my mind flashed our saying, *friendly fir or spiky spruce*? Definitely not a spiky spruce, the needles were too soft. A fir then? What about hemlock? Yew? I leaned farther in to the knobby bark of the trunk and my thumb pressed into a gob of sticky sap. I rolled the resin between thumb and forefinger, then brought my hand to my nose.

Oh! I was grinning like a jolly elf. I pulled a pinch of needles off a branch, crushed them between my fingers, rolled them with the sap and brought them back to my nose. This smell meant happiness. This smell evoked the time of year when for brief moments or entire days, home and family meant comfort and joy. Christmas morning: snow falling outside, paper birch fire crackling in the cast iron woodstove, and colorful packages under the tree. *This tree*. Balsam fir!

I stood smiling with sappy fingers planted under my nostrils until Leda's giggle snapped me back from my olfactory memories, the crackling fire and Nat King Cole song in my head supplanted by the chortling chickadees, nuthatches, and grey squirrels of the August woodland. A slow descending loon laugh echoed from Half Moon Pond.

I wasn't just comfortable in the woods; I was downright giddy. Environmental education invited me to connect with the natural world in a way I hadn't before. The science taught me that every rock, tree, and bird had an interesting origin and rich life history. My senses allowed me to experience them, intimately, to absorb them into my own life history. The comfortable woods were becoming a community of friends who fascinated and delighted me, yet demanded nothing.

We continued on. Over roots, under branches, around boulders and up, up, up, my body told me. As the ground leveled, I began to hear rushing water. Not the gentle lapping of the pond, but the agitated gurgling, sloshing, splashing of the river. We had to be nearing the Nubanusit, a name that hints at the story of the people who came before. Like the humble Mount Skatutakee or more imposing Monadnock of our skyline, this land was continually whispering stories to anyone willing to listen.

Down, down, down we descended toward the rushing sound, until Leda sat me on a flat rock to wait while she walked away for a minute. I could smell the river then, almost taste it, the organic boggy sedges, rushes, and shrubs on the banks and the cleaner almost metallic waters rolling over rocks in the middle.

"Ok, hold out both hands and don't make any noise."

I heard another blindfolded person guided to sit nearby, who was then instructed to use his/her sense of touch to try to decipher who I was. I knew the game – another icebreaker. I offered up my hands to this stranger to explore in the odd comfort of anonymous intimacy.

What stories are concealed in my hands?

The grace of twice weekly ballet classes from the age of five to sixteen. Wrists that learned to relax and fingers to curl softly away from whichever direction my arms moved, "Like swans! No sharp edges!" chirped my severe British ballet teacher. Flowing through space as if gliding in water.

Scribbling love letters in purple pen, passing origami notes in the hallways, and holding the pink plastic phone to my sweaty ear, twirling the phone cord for hours. Learning a body different from my own. The downy hairs on the back of his neck, the lines of muscle along his spine, the points of his narrow hipbones. The mutual embrace of first love, a love that would last forever.

Fingernails painted black, pressing the emptiness in my chest after he left me. Covering my ears, trying to block out the screaming fights down the hall, hoping this father wouldn't hurt my mother, hoping this father wouldn't leave too. Fists clenched with a smoldering rage I did not understand.

Accidental Swiss Army knife cut, deep in the cartilage of my right index finger. The surprising relief of it, anger and grief draining away with the blood dripping on the purple carpet. The power in it.

Cutting. Bleeding. Leaving marks on my legs, stomach, chest, arms, and hands. Broken glass, serrated steak knives, razor blades. Knuckles raked across brick walls or punched until swollen twice their size.

Wounds too numerous to hide, wounds that betrayed. Hands clasped before a therapist who knew my therapist mother and therapist stepfather, telling me to stop hurting those around me. Hands at my sides, obedient.

These are the fires of my origins.

The blindfolded stranger let go my hands and stayed silent, as instructed.

"Okay! It's our turn!" The excitement was audible in Leda's voice as she pulled me to my feet, so I knew I was in for something big. The others who earlier had scattered into the forest all seemed to have arrived at this waiting place but were leaving again, whispered instructions barely audible and voices growing distant.

But. No footsteps! Where did they go?

My turn.

With the river on my right, I followed Leda along the bank to what I felt with my foot was the base of a large tree. Taking my hands, Leda placed the left one on rough wooden steps at knee level and the other slightly above on a steel cable secured around the tree.

"You are going to stand on this cable," she whispered close to my ear. "There is another cable above that you will hold onto. Use the pine tree to climb up. Once you are up, you will walk along the cables for a bit until you reach a vertical cable. Only then can you take your blindfold off, but don't make any noise."

Now I was scared.

I climbed the three steps, hugging the tree, and stepped up onto the cable. It wobbled under my weight and I struggled to steady it. Once my right hand found the upper cable I grabbed it with both hands and gripped so tightly my fingernails dug into my palms. *The wire will hold me. The wire will hold me?*

This is an activity we will be doing with kids, right? So it can't be dangerous, right? Those aren't my knees shaking the cable, are they?

And I moved. First one foot, then the other. One scarred hand, then the other. Slowly, steadily, I slid along into the void. My fists on the wire the only things saving me from what was surely an abyss below.

Though I was quiet, my mind shouted instructions from opposing sides of a raging war.

Cheat! Look down under the blindfold and make sure you're safe!

Relax! You trust these people. Enjoy the experience. Breathe.

You're going to fall off! You're going to be the only one who messes up and falls off and ruins it for everyone!

Listen to the birds, the water...

The water! Sounds like rapids! You're going to die!

No. This doesn't feel like death. This feels like life, magnified.

I kept my eyes closed. I slid along the cables. I breathed. My heart thumped. All the hairs on my body stood at attention.

What's this? My foot met something solid. My hand found it. It was the vertical cable, between the two.

I pulled off my blindfold.

I blinked away the blur, squinted in the dazzling brightness and saw everything, all at once. Water shimmered jade green and gold in the afternoon light of an azure sky. Spearmint-colored reeds waved in the shallows and silver minnows darted among them. Scattered rocks downriver curled water into frothy white eddies then sent it gurgling on its way. I was in the middle of it all, perched three feet above and halfway across the lazy river.

I am Dorothy and this is surely the Emerald City. Was my world always this stunning, this marvelous?

It was. It is.

My knees were shaking again, though no longer from fear of the unknown. I could see through the satin-smooth Nubanusit that the sandy river bottom was no more than four feet below the surface. I was safe. The remaining butterflies in my stomach fluttered away.

Among the needled pines and leafy chartreuse alders and birches of the far bank I could see those who went before me, perched on granite boulders waving and silently cheering in shared elation. I looked back to watch Leda hop up on the wire and breeze toward me in red fleece and fraying blue jeans, chestnut eyes sparkling and cheeks dimpled in a wide grin. I continued across and jumped down to await the final blind crossings. One by one, my coworkers pulled off blindfolds and brief looks of confusion transformed to the innocent glee of toddlers. The elation of a child who's been handed a new puppy.

Once my last coworker hugged one arm to the cable and pulled the blindfold down around his neck, grinning like a fairytale child on Christmas morning, we could all finally give voice to our merriment. We leapt off boulders, hooting and hollering like hyenas.

We'd been handed the gift of newness, an adrenaline-boosted fresh perspective of our known world, an experience we couldn't wait to share with kids and adults alike over the coming year.

But while the blind river crossing might be the story we told the most from outdoor school, my favorite stories were the quiet ones, the humble ones, the stories told by individual rocks, trees, rivers, and birds. The stories that might be found in books but are best experienced with your body. Look, listen, smell, reach out and explore. Ask, research, and ask again.

In touching the earth, my own stories shifted. I began to feel less like a confused human among humans and more like an individual among myriad individuals, one bundle of stories on an earth full of stories. In reaching for stone, wood, water, and feather, I found my own edges softening, scars fading.

Later that week I stood, hands at my sides, with this new batch of environmental educators. The line on our schedule read "wildlife ecology," and we were beginning with birds. In the afternoon light through sugar maples and beech trees, black-capped chickadees snatched sunflower seeds, one at a time, from a small platform in a clearing. We took turns observing them through binoculars and chatted about bird behavior.

Then came a surprise. Our instructor, Kelly, held out a bag of seed and asked each of us to take a handful. Eyes glinting, she told us that one at a time we could try to feed the birds. From our hands.

Really? This was possible? We were allowed to do this? It would work, she told us, if we were calm and still and let them trust us.

When it was my turn, I stepped toward the clearing, gliding with the smoothness of a ballet-trained body. Slowly. Evenly. Like a swan – no sharp edges. My right arm floated up... wrist rotated... palm up... fingers curled open to expose the seeds.

I relaxed my shoulders, exhaled, and said in my mind, *Trust me.*

Chickadee-dee-dee-dee-dee. They were talking it over.

Then, tiny feet and toenails light as paperclips touched down on my palm, and a peck of a beak to a seed and it was gone. Then another. And again, as the seeds disappeared one by one.

When the last seed was lifted away I closed my tingling hand and held tight a feeling that wasn't like emptiness at all. It was more like a cooling salve on a burn, a kiss on a wound to make it better. A gift I would carry long after I moved on from those New Hampshire woods, like granite in ice.

Bite Marks

I don't remember the pain. Pain's funny like that. I do remember the six stings of Novocain in my forehead and what was left of my cheek. How my face refused to numb on command. I remember the fat needle of morphine in the vein below my bicep, and insisting I could still feel everything. I was never good at not feeling.

I'd been waiting for more than an hour in the ER for the plastic surgeon to arrive, supine on white paper under white lights with the whitecoats and my mother, and I had to pee. Use a bedpan they said. No way I said. I'm an adult and I can walk to the bathroom. They said move slowly, the morphine. Don't look in the mirror, they said.

Four hands pulled me to my feet, and when the room stopped undulating I shuffled down the hall to the bathroom. I looked in the mirror.

My eyes stared out from behind a Halloween mask, chunky

red and white strips of gore instead of my left cheek, teeth and gums showing through a hole in my chin. As my mind struggled to make sense of what I saw, a wave of nausea sideswiped me. I white-knuckled the porcelain sink for a moment then abandoned the mirror, found the toilet, managed to pee and not vomit, and shuffled past the mirror back to the ER. That time I avoided my reflection.

On the adorable meter, Wheaten terrier puppies are animals most likely to elicit spontaneous high-pitched baby talk from the gruffest of humans. Perfectly puppy proportioned with round, squat faces, dark eyes, and vanilla-chocolate swirled waves of hair, they are little cowlicky teddy bears. They mature into wavy blonde adult teddy bears, medium sized dogs resembling meticulously coifed sheepdogs or "Return of the Jedi" Ewoks. Like many terriers, Wheatens were bred as generalist farm dogs, human companions who guarded the home and kept down the rats. My parents selected the breed because they are known to be excellent family dogs – cheerful, social, and great with kids.

Brandi was our second Wheaten, purchased from a breeder and acquired as soon as she was weaned. I helped train her, spoiled her with table scraps and a seat on the good couch. I did my share of leashed walks in the neighborhood and throwing the ball in the yard. Brandi was a little needy, a little high-strung as terriers are known to be. She showed some signs of separation anxiety, barking and dancing circles whenever we left, and she occasionally growled if anyone came too near her food dish at feeding time. Garden variety dog neuroses, nothing that two shrinks and their teenaged girls couldn't handle. She fit right in with our family.

In the spirit of family pets everywhere, Brandi was the one who was always there, always happy to see me when I came home from high school, or later, from college. When a boyfriend broke up with me, when my sister and I decided that we hated each other, or when my mother and stepfather were fighting, there was a soft smiling animal to remind me of sweetness. If I was feeling alone in the world, gloomy and sighing, Brandi would sit by my side and sigh with me. I'd look into those teddy bear eyes looking back at me, and I'd feel loved.

When the charged emotions of adolescence swirled into that overwhelming combination of seething anger, anxiety, and grief beyond logic that made me want to run off to the woods never to return, there was a wolf's descendant to remind me that I was an animal too, and maybe I was just a little wilder than most.

Even after I moved away to college, visiting home on breaks and in summers meant visiting Brandi. When I graduated and moved two hours north, I still came home regularly for my mother's home cooking, a washing machine that didn't require quarters, and to pet my dog.

One summer afternoon when I was twenty-three, I arrived home for a weekend visit. My sister was away for the summer, my stepfather still at work, but my mother was around somewhere. When I walked in the door and threw my duffle bag to the floor all I saw was Brandi, sitting quietly in the kitchen doorway. *Braaaandeeee* I yelled and trotted up to her, then sat down in front of her to say hi.

I reach for her.

She growls softly, a faraway guttural sound like someone drowning. I hear her but don't have time to react. It isn't a warning anyway, it is the beginning of something already in motion.

Her jaws seize my face and her teeth sink deeply as if trying to devour me whole like a snake. She holds on. She keeps holding on as I rip my face away. Her top teeth shred the muscle and nerve of my left cheek and her bottom teeth slash my lower lip into my gums. I won't remember the pain. I will remember my scream, and that I wrap my arms around my head to keep her from attacking again. I crumple and cower on the floor, flinching as something touches my shoulder but it is just my mother. I don't know where Brandi is.

Let me see, the therapist taking over, Mom's voice firm and strong. *Okay, we need to get you to the hospital.* Does she look at Brandi? Does Brandi look at us? I can't see her anymore.

During the forty-five minute drive I hold a washcloth to my face, suck in air and kick the floor of the car as my mother curses red lights, tells me to hang in there. Her voice no longer calm, her voice shrill with motherworry. I'm quiet. I tell her it's okay. I won't remember the pain, but I will remember it fills my world so full there is room for nothing else. No dog, no family, no blood-soaked washcloth holding my face together, no emotion, no past or future. There is only my body, alive in the now. Pain obliterates all else.

In the emergency room I felt the doctor tug at my cheek, caught glimpses of flaps of skin in his gloved hands as he attempted to put the puzzle back together. Plastic surgeons are artists; they think more about the finished product than just closing wounds, which is why we'd waited for him. I watched his squint-eyed concentration as he told me he was making most of the stitch lines in the natural creases and laugh lines of my face so that when they faded they'd be less noticeable. When he finished he stood back, looking pleased. He asked if he could take some pictures for his portfolio. You'll heal well, he said.

At home, my stepfather greeted me with open arms. But not Brandi. After receiving the call from my mother, Dad had taken her to the vet for a lethal injection. When he'd returned home from work to take her away, how did she act? Did he stay with her when the vet did it, or did he leave her there? I never did ask him. Maybe because I knew those weren't the real questions.

After swallowing four ibuprofen to buffer my diminishing

morphine haze, I climbed the stairs to bed. My bathroom mirror showed me a new mask, a patchwork Frankenface. I counted the loops in the swollen redness, knowing that whenever stitches are involved, people always want to know how many. I lost count at forty and, considering the hidden ones inside my mouth and in the muscle of my cheek, I decided that "more than fifty" would suffice.

The next morning, one fitful sleep's distance from what had happened, I started asking why. When a trusted friend or family member suddenly turns on you, attacks or physically injures you, you assume the usual causes. But Brandi came from an upstanding family line, was never abused, and showed no signs of mental illness. Was she jealous of me with my mother? Protective of her food? Asserting dominance over me when I'd made myself submissive? How could any of these explanations justify the severity of her reaction? How could I possibly have brought that on myself? As the pain subsided and my face started to heal, another part of me remained wounded.

I sought out statistics. Found ones that say dogs don't bite unless provoked. Found ones that say they do. I looked to biologists, behaviorists and psychologists, found multitudes of reasons and similar stories. But none of them gave me clarity. Brandi and I are statistics now, too. My own dog attacked me, tried to tear my face off, and we killed her for it.

For months I had no feeling in the left side of my face, my expressions the lopsided droop of a stroke victim amidst the angry crimson swell of new scars. Thankfully free from the extreme self-consciousness of adolescence, I was nevertheless a timid young adult with mediocre self-esteem. My new face made me want to flee to a cave. Still, the stares, double-takes and, once, outright laughter were nothing compared with the verbal reactions of those bold enough to speak.

What happened to your face?!
Dog bite.

What did you do? Nothing? You must have done something. Dogs don't just bite people for no reason. Then it must have been mistreated. What kind of dog, a pit bull? What did the owner do? You should sue them. What happened to the dog?

With each replay of that conversation I sank deeper into the reality of the incomprehensible truth. My dog. I don't know why.

I would give anything to know Brandi's story. Did she revert to wildness, some overwhelming combination of seething anger, anxiety, and grief beyond logic? Did she sense something in me that I didn't? Something broken, something dangerous?

After she did it, did she feel regret? Did she understand how she had hurt me, want to take it back the way the rest of my family did when we lashed out at one another? Or did she feel satisfaction in giving in to a long-repressed desire? Did she relish the taste of my blood?

I abandoned the truth, started lying. *The neighbor's dog. Nothing, just went crazy. Yes, must have been abused. They put him to sleep, thank god.*

And suddenly, dogs were everywhere. Every outdoor space, public or private, and many indoor ones. Big ones, small ones, loud ones, silent ones, but all of them with mouths open, teeth exposed. Everywhere, the unpredictable beasts. Everywhere, danger. The first time one of them ran toward me barking I was electrocuted. My face burned and body froze, heart bounded and breath whistled through my constricted throat. My trembling hands clawed at my face.

Cynophobia: an exaggerated, irrational, or otherwise abnormal fear of dogs. Exaggerated, maybe. But irrational?

If it had been a wild animal, I would have understood. Wild animals need to find food, protect their young, protect themselves from what they don't understand. Wild animals are beyond the good and evil of humans. Nature, my sanctuary, may be a place of harsh realities, of predator/prey, life and death, but it's a place that makes sense to me.

I'd always thought that people are the only ones capable of actual cruelty, who can consciously choose to betray trust, cause harm, attack or kill. People—most of us—are aware of what we're doing. We know better. Yet we continue to hurt each other. Again and again.

And dogs? Man's best friend? Did Brandi know better?

I think she did.

For more than 10,000 years, dogs have been evolving at our sides. Scientists now think that early dogs domesticated themselves, not the other way around. A few bold wolves slunk close to our cooking fires, started hanging around our farms, fought their wolfish instincts to seek the eyes of humans for mutual benefit. Will work for food.

A recent study reported in *Science Magazine* found that this coevolution has gone so far that when dogs seek eye contact with their humans, this mutual gaze releases the same bonding hormone—oxytocin—released between human mother and baby. Not just in the human, but the dog. There is no such phenomenon among wolves.

Dogs are no more wild than we are. I may not ever understand why Brandi looked me in the eye and attacked, but I don't think it was latent wildness. I believe it was something far more sinister. Her humanity.

Scars fade. That plastic surgeon? He did do an excellent job. A few of the scars are noticeable – a white line here, a slight fold there – but most of them have disappeared into the lines of an aging face. Despite warnings to the contrary, my facial nerves have fully regenerated. So much so that if I touch my tongue to the roof of my mouth I can feel it in my cheek. I was never good at not feeling.

Phobias fade, too. Twenty years of mostly positive

experiences with canines retrained my autonomic nervous system to listen to reason. Observe and react if necessary, not the other way around. But the guttural growl of an angry dog will still jolt me, and even a known, friendly dog's jaws near my face will quicken my breath and start my hands trembling.

I don't remember the pain of teeth tearing flesh, but I do remember what it feels like to be attacked by a friend. What I still feel, even now, is the sorrow of a broken heart.

Hand Wing

Your entire body fit in the palm of my hand. I could feel your pebble-sized heart racing through the warmth of your soft brown fur. My fingers curled around you firmly but loosely so as not to crush you, your head the only visible part of you peeking out from near my thumb. Your mouth gaped open in what I realized must have been aggression but in such small scale appeared more like a cartoonish grin. You were particularly feisty, I realized, because your swollen belly and chest told me you were going to be a mama. I ran my thumb along the top of your head between your ears, which calmed you, a little. I was completely smitten.

With my other hand I chose a metal band from the professor's bag and snugged it tightly around the meaty part of your upper arm – your new jewelry, an arm cuff with a scientific number on it in case you are found again. Then I opened my right hand and waited. You crawled with your elbows to the edge of my palm and hung down from your feet for a minute, shivering, warming up. Then you spread your leathery wings and flew, back into the night.

~

Bats are not flying mice. They are not yellow-toothed gnawing mammals of the Rodentia order, but flying mammals of Chiroptera, meaning "hand-wing." Peel back their skins and see they more closely resemble us than mice. Tiny human-proportioned skeletons with snouts and tails, five-fingered hands, palms open. We primates share a shrew-like ancestor.

Watch their extended families, sophisticated social relationships like wolf packs. A mother births and attentively cares for one poorly developed pup per year, nursing from pectoral breasts. When mothers go out to hunt, babysitters or grandmothers keep watch. Elders may live into their thirties.

Bats are at home on every continent except Antarctica. Some dive for fish like osprey, stalk frogs, prey on scorpions and centipedes, and yes, some thirst for blood. Others nibble fruit, sip nectar, or nose pollen, cultivating food crops such as bananas, mangos, avocados, and figs. Like tequila? Thank long-nosed bats for the success of agave plants.

Most of our North American bats dine on insects only, acting as nocturnal counterparts of birds like warblers and swallows. Mosquitoes are most active at night, and one little brown bat can eat 1,200 of them in one hour. Insectivorous bats are also important predators of crop-eating moths. According to Bat Conservation International, "throughout the United States, scientists estimate, bats are worth more than $3.7 billion a year in reduced crop damage and pesticide use."

~

Sixteen of us lived in one 1700s New Hampshire farmhouse. But we were all twenty-something environmental education interns who didn't mind the summer camp feel of a bustling home jam-packed with milk crates of long underwear and raingear, hiking boots and Tevas, and granola bars in Tupperware because of the mice.

Sometimes we minded the mice. Like the time a mouse ran across my face at 2 a.m. and I freaked out and duct taped every possible hole where it might have entered. There are a lot of holes in a 1700s New Hampshire farmhouse.

In the common room, three couches and four easy chairs backed up against bicycles, cross country skis, camping gear, and climbing ropes hanging from the ceiling and tucked into corners. Sometimes at night when we were watching a movie and the lights were out, a bat would squeeze through a crack between the ceiling and attic crawl space and fly around the room. Though startling at first, we resisted the urge to shriek and wave our hands and chase it out with a broom, because that would be bad form for an environmental educator. Instead we opened the door and eventually the bat flew outside. This happened so often that we all got used to it, and sometimes nobody bothered to get up to open the door until the movie ended.

"Hey bat. How nice of you to drop in!" It flew around, squeaking and clicking, or landed on the tire of a hanging bike, or occasionally found its way back up through the cracks to the attic. It didn't eat our food or poop in the common room, so we didn't mind the bat. Bats in our belfry? Sure, why not?

~

Bats are not blind. Blind as a bat means not blind at all. They see as well as or better than we do, but even the best eyes don't work in complete darkness. Whereas most nocturnal mammals rely mainly on hearing, insectivorous bats boast a sixth sense. Super heroes with magic powers, they wield ultrasonic pulses that reverberate to ridged satellite dish ears and noses to create mind maps and keep track of very small, very fast prey. Echolocation is rare in the animal world, shared only by toothed whales (including dolphins), two genera of shrews, two types of cave-dwelling birds, and industrious blind humans.

An insectivorous bat in your belfry or fluttering about your yard at night has no interest in you or your hair. She may, however, enjoy a meal of the mosquitoes buzzing around your head. Be still so she can keep from colliding with you. Listen to her click and buzz, the barely audible evidence of a secret language. Clicks increase in frequency when she is about to feed.

~

I scrambled up a bright snowy hillside and crawled through a hole into a dank, dripping bat cave. Or hibernaculum, to be exact. After the biting frosty air of New Hampshire winter outside, the relative warmth and humidity of the cave washed over me. My lungs expanded and nose-hairs thawed in the mineral moisture of a place where no plants grew.

At first all I saw were the little clouds each exhale puffed into the beam of my headlamp. I blinked, widened my vision and the walls came into view. I reached out and swiped a finger along gritty brown rock. The cave was a long-ago abandoned silver mine shaft, so the narrow passageway was about as tall as an average man, the chiseled stone walls only inches from me on all sides.

I extended a leg forward, testing the depth of a puddle with the tip of my boot. A couple inches of water on solid rock. Shuffle, step, splash. Above me, dozens of fist-sized brown bodies adorned the walls, glistening with dew. No silver remained in the mine, but our shining treasure was there.

I caught up with the other biologists and we moved deeper into the darkness. On my clipboard I ticked off hash marks in different species columns as they whispered: *Eptesicus fuscus. Myotis lucifugus. Perimyotis subflavus...* Shuffle, step, splash. Drip. Drip.

I took my own additional microclimate measurements of temperature, humidity, and wind speed every five-meter interval in the cave. In each section I recorded which species were present. For my master's thesis I was trying to determine how particular hibernating bats are when choosing their roosting sites, and whether this differs by species.

A northern myotis hung at eye level, its body so close we could see tiny toes gripping a wrinkle in the rock, toenails glistening like sugar crystals. Long time bat lovers and more recent converts, we exchanged toothy grins as we lingered in the tunnel. But our body heat and head lamps were warming the cave, and a few bats had woken up and started flying around. We hurried to finish collecting our data and leave them in peace.

~

Because of the metabolic demands of flight, bats have evolved unique thermoregulation mechanisms. Rather than maintaining a relatively constant body temperature through food and exercise like other mammals, bats also choose environments to suit their needs, like reptiles. When pregnant and caring for young, mothers choose warm attics and barns so they don't deplete their energy staying warm. In North American winters when food is scarce, some bats migrate to warmer locations while others hibernate. Hibernators choose locations with microclimates that allow them to use the least amount of energy possible to stay alive until warmth and bugs return in spring. This differs by species.

High metabolic demands, low reproduction rates, and a

tendency to gather in large numbers make bat populations particularly vulnerable to disturbance and disease. Even though a fungal disease known as white-nose syndrome is killing bats by the thousands, humans are still the number-one threat to bats. We set fires in hibernacula, seal caves shut, and tear down old barns. We exterminate whole maternity colonies from our attics.

~

Bats are outcasts, misfits, outsiders. Their association with night and darkness has long relegated them in folklore to the realm of death or the underworld. Angels wear the white feathers of doves; the devil wears bat wings. Bats inhabit our world, but on the periphery, the fringes, the places we fear to go. Steeples, attics, barns, caves, hollow trees and tombs. They hang upside-down and use streams as flyways, further connections with the underworld.

Bats are vampires. Vampires are bats. Never mind that Old World vampire myths appeared millennia before the earliest reports of actual blood-drinking animals. Never mind that only three of the 1,000 bat species feed solely on blood. Or that the blood-borne mammalian disease rabies is far more common in raccoons, foxes and dogs, and that rabid bats rarely bite, but usually just die.

And never mind that vampire bats are among the most intelligent, social, and altruistic of all bat species. They adopt orphans. They share food with less fortunate, even unrelated bats. They groom each other, like gorillas. But if you choose to camp in the open on a Peruvian mountainside, a little vampire might use her razor-sharp incisors to make an incision on your big toe, her saliva keeping your blood from coagulating, and lap up your blood like a kitten. It could happen.

~

I was not on a Peruvian mountainside. I was watching the last rays of late summer sun fade behind the Douglas firs of Oregon's Estacada Lake as a fisherman packed up his gear and a freshly caught rainbow trout. I tipped my ranger hat to him and led my group out onto the wooden dock. Families wired on s'mores and clutching flashlights followed my lead and started scanning the skies.

I thought of you, my first chiropteran crush. Your swollen belly, the soft fur between your ears. I wondered about your children, and your children's children. You should have been a grandmother by then. Probably, you weren't.

But because of you, I was standing in that polyester ranger uniform on a state park dock at dusk. Because of you I was driven to help those campground visitors make their own connections, form positive memories to turn scary strangers into friends. I knew I couldn't protect you from everyone, from everything. But as I gazed at pockets of light on the water from the rising moon, I wished that just this group of families, these parents and children, would fall in love as I had.

And then I heard them. A few clicks, a faint squeak. The flickery flutter of paper-thin wings.

"I saw one!" a girl squealed and tugged my sleeve.

"I saw it too!" her father said, eyes as wide.

"Did you see that?!" others joined in.

It was a warm night. The mosquitoes, gnats, and moths were out in full force and with them, the night hunters. Darting over the water, diving under the dock, and zipping just above our heads they put on a good show. Little brown bats, big brown bats, and maybe even the rare, bunny-eared, Townsend's big-eared bats who raised their babies in a nearby barn.

I was ecstatic. And I was relieved. We weren't yelling, weren't throwing rocks, weren't running away. We were smiling, welcoming, accepting of the furry beasts. We were all there together, getting along. We were more than our prejudices, greater than our ignorance, wiser than our fears.

World peace, one bat at a time.

Miracles, Frozen

According to my nose, winter renders three stages of cold. Stage one – constant, copious running that quickly saturates any hanky and leaves me wiping with shirt sleeves like a child. Stage two – snot thickened to molasses, hanging by a single clear drop from the tip of my nose, but I can no longer feel the tip of my nose. Stage three – mucus membranes shut down entirely, but each exhalation's slight humidity causes nose hairs to thaw and refreeze with every in and out.

It may have been early March in southern New Hampshire, but it was stage three cold outside. My thighs were already numb despite long underwear, fleece pants, and my brisk pace on the wooded trail. I welcomed the cold, rubbed pink fingers together to feel the biting sting. Wiggled snow-boot-cramped toes and kicked at a patch of snow flecked with snow fleas. It didn't help. The grief lodged in my chest was still there.

Graduate school in environmental studies was supposed to

teach me about ecology – the study of connections – so I could better understand the natural world that I loved. To train me as a naturalist, a field researcher, and a wildlife manager, so I could get a fun job working outside. I was getting all of that, but with it came the weight of how much harm we've caused. How bad things have really gotten.

Sure, I had known of the destruction of clear-cuts, the food chain effects of pesticides, the inevitability of the end of oil. I was a member of the Sierra Club and Save the Whales. In high school I joined the Environmental Action Group and wrote my senior term paper on the history of the environmental movement up to that point in 1990. The earth had specific wounds and the good people of the world were working to heal them. I was going to become one of *those* people.

But now, I had statistics. Now, I had projections. Understanding the connections meant understanding the reverberating consequences of billions more greedy hominids than our planet can sustain. There were no discrete wounds. My own species was a cancer. Stage four. And Band-Aids weren't enough.

I stopped, my scuffling footsteps still. The quiet, louder. I exhaled a silver cloud. Next to the trail the earth dipped into a smooth depression the size of a kiddie pool. I waded in and lay down on my back, frozen nose pointed at the ebony spears of leafless trees against a pewter sky.

Maybe I would stay there. Give in and freeze. I never was a fighter. Impending destruction or even significant conflict make me stutter, shake, cower. Where other people are energized to stand up and fight, I crumple like a fainting goat. I turtle.

Icy snowflakes drifted down, slowly at first, wafting like milkweed. Then harder, faster, so that I had to squint through the onslaught. I began to see three distinct walls of snow, each moving a different direction at varying distances from me, and finally I had to close my eyes. Maybe I would have stayed there.

Except.

Except something soft and wet, warmer. The snow was turning to rain. Mother Nature does that sometimes, switches gears just when it seems like winter will never cease. Suddenly there's spring, slushy and grey and full of promise. In that woodland depression, snowmelt would collect with rain, and the empty bowl would soon be full again. A vernal pool, an ephemeral wetland swimming with life. Life that was there all along. I don't mean the quiet ones, the rooted leafy green ones. I mean, specifically, the tiniest of the local frogs, *Pseudacris crucifer*, spring peepers.

Nestled under leaves or tucked beneath logs all winter long were frogs the size of cotton balls, light as nickels. Severe cold stimulates a chemical change that gives them blood-sugar levels high enough to kill a person, but which act as frog antifreeze to protect inner cells from freezing solid and cell walls from being destroyed by ice crystals. Little froggie slushies. When it warms up again, their bodies reverse the process, no harm done.

It will take a miracle to survive what we've done to our planet. But aren't there miracles all around us? In that very vernal pool, after the first heavy spring rain, a hundred tiny miracles would open up their mouths, expand their throats and sing. Not the song of a warm-blooded, feathered animal boasting of his winter in the bountiful tropics. But the song of a delicate, thin-skinned amphibian who began life in water and changed from the inside out to be able to live on land. The song of an animal who knows what it is to lie still for three months with ice crystals in his veins. *That* song.

I wish I could say that on that cold March day I just thought of the frogs and my grief for the earth went away. I wish I could say that I found the strength to stand up and fight or at least the hope to believe that this beautiful world will somehow remain as it is, but I can't. I didn't. I knew too much.

Spring comes earlier every year, and warmth doesn't always mean rebirth. Too much warmth, too fast, will destroy the delicate balance of frog and vernal pool and cause equally disruptive ripples throughout the forest ecosystem. The erratic weather patterns, catastrophic storms, and rising sea levels that accompany the changing climate will cause additional stress and destruction. What miracles could survive this, and what will that survival look like? Will there still be singing?

My nose was running now, joining slushy rivulets of rain dribbling down my neck. It was time to move. My body chemistry isn't as advanced as a spring peeper, and hypothermia would not be a good way to go. I rolled to my side, up to hands and knees, and then to my feet. Brushed myself off and jumped up and down a couple times to get the blood moving. I may not be a fighter, but I'm not a quitter.

I continued my walk in the woods I'd come to know so well. This was the trail where I observed plant communities for botany class. To the south was the riverside where I watched birds for ornithology. To the north, the beaver pond I studied for wildlife and forest management. I was heading toward the meadow edge where I'd donned snowshoes and tracked mammals for natural resource inventory.

A walk in the woods would never again be just a walk in the woods. Names, life histories, and ecological relationships announced themselves from every direction, my brain eagerly reinforcing information that all our ancestors knew, had to know to survive, but these days few of us ever learn.

This forest wasn't here two hundred years ago. This was a sheep farm – grass fields, a grove of apple trees, and a lattice of stone walls. No oaks, no maples, no sycamores or birches, no hemlocks. No vernal pools and no spring peepers. Not here.

The old-growth forest that stood before the European settler colonialists clear-cut it for farm fields and timber was gone; that was still true. But this was a forest teeming with life, not a trampled pasture with very little. Not a parking lot with none. What interested me were not the socioeconomic reasons why we'd left the land alone, such as farming moving west or New Englanders moving to the cities. What interested me was what happened here when we did leave. Every tree, every nesting bird, and every frog told a story that was something like hope. Ephemeral, maybe, precarious, definitely, but right then, that's all I had.

I was nearing the edge of the forest and could see the yellow porch light of my cabin in the otherwise gray scale dusk. I thought I saw a shadow move in front of it, but decided it was just the trees in the wind. When I got to the edge of the trail, however, fresh tracks in old snow told a different story. Triangular palm pad, four toe pads, and sharp claws. They looked like dog tracks, but I didn't have a dog, and no dogs lived nearby. These tracks cut a straight line from the meadow into the forest, crossing a stone wall away from the trail. Coyote.

Two hundred years ago, coyotes wouldn't have been here either. Not this kind. Just as a new and different forest came after old growth was cut and farmers moved on, so a new canine arrived. A hybrid of the dominant wolf (nearly extirpated in the area by nervous sheep farmers) and smaller, scruffier coyote (moving east from the Great Plains), this adaptable subspecies has qualities of each. The size and hunting prowess to take down deer and small moose, and the wily skills of a true generalist omnivore happy to subsist on fruit, vegetable gardens, rats, mice, carrion, pet food left outside, pets left outside, compost piles, and human trash.

Later that night, after the rain turned back to snow, a pack of eastern coyotes yipped and yowled and wailed, wild echoes that made me grin and shiver though I was no longer cold. A song equal parts wolf and scruffy scavenger, equal parts mournful and triumphant. A sound like hope.

My foray into environmental science wouldn't turn me into an activist, or even, really, a scientist. But it would serve to deepen my emotional connections with the natural world. Time spent in nature would at times console, inspire, or simply remind me to pick myself up and keep moving. It would keep me from getting so wrapped up in statistics and predictions that I forgot what it felt like to lay on my back on the frozen earth and feel the snow turn to rain.

I would begin to seek others like me, those who loved the earth not simply from a utilitarian or even aesthetic drive, but with a sentimental passion. Others who knew the names and connections among the lives around us as well as how precious they are, miraculous even. John Muir, Edward Abbey, Terry Tempest Williams. Those who understood delight in nature as deeply as they understood the science. Henry David Thoreau, Annie Dillard, Mary Oliver. The professors, naturalists, and other mentors right in front of me who helped remind me to feel, smell, taste, watch, and listen to the earth. Spring Peeper. Coyote.

The earth needs fighters, of course it does. But it also needs songs. The songs that may be tinged with grief, guilt, or righteous anger, but always, always bursting with jubilant awe of the little miracles that somehow persist, even thrive. Frog songs. Coyote songs. Those are the songs I would learn, the way I would keep from freezing. So one day, when I am ready, I might tilt back my scruffy head and sing out my own mournful triumph.

Part 2: Migrations

Behind Bars

At the end of my evening shift at the Beans & Brews coffeehouse, I put up my hood and shuffled steel-toed boots four blocks south to the other end of Liberty Park. There I unlocked three padlocks and muscled open the fifteen-foot, barbed-wire-enforced gate just enough to slip through.

Gate locked behind me, I breathed easier and settled into my senses to enjoy the walk through the 'hood to my shack. The only lights spilled in from the park outside, but I knew my way in the shadows. Between the hours of 6 p.m. and 7 a.m., this exclusive Salt Lake City community belonged only to me and a bevy of birds.

As I crunched the gravel pathway between the raptor cages, the owls always let me know they were awake. The docile great horned owl swiveled her head and beamed yellow eyes my way. I hooted a greeting, knowing she would answer. "Who's awake? Meee tooooooo," in owlish. A more pleasant welcome home than I could expect from the barn owl across the path, who would sit calmly on the glove for public education programs but raged in his enclosure. Like clockwork, he shrieked like a banshee (or do banshees shriek like barn owls?) and flew at the cage as I passed, sharp talons gleaming through the cracks. "You're okay— it's just me," I cooed.

Once through the owls I entered the public area of the aviary where a variety of exotic ducks, geese, peacocks, and other non-flighted and wing-clipped birds had the run of the place outside the cages. I'd learned quickly where the geese laid their eggs to avoid being startled by hissing ankle-biting parents as they chased me away. Aside from the occasional mallard snicker or goose kerfuffle from the pond, the diurnal residents were quiet as I clomped the path home. If I spied any walnuts fallen from the tree, I made sure to crunch them under my boots, knowing the peacocks would delight in them come daytime.

These almost-free birds seemed to lead a comfortable life, food coming to them every day, protected behind the outer walls as I was. That is, as long as they managed not to blunder over the fence that enclosed the eagles, flightless birds once injured in the wild. I did get a secret pleasure when it happened though, never begrudging our alter-abled residents a rare kill and fresh goose for dinner. I am sure it beat the cold dead chickens their keepers served up.

Safely through the waterfowl and past the eagles, I walked up the path to my two-room office-turned-cabin, nearly getting a mouthful of peacock feathers from the bird perched at face level on my front gate. Inside, I listened to a few last quacks, whistles, and hoots before we all settled in for the night. I slept well there, beneath the pair of albino peacocks nestled on my roof.

Tracy Aviary hired me as their first zookeeper intern, wherein a novice could gain experience in aviculture and be paid in "housing" they were paying for anyway. I'd hit that mid-twenties period when you suddenly realize there is a whole country out there and you must go explore it, immediately. Coming from small-town New Hampshire, a bird zoo in a big city in the arid Rocky Mountains sounded like a grand adventure.

Like the country girl I once was, I could expect to awaken at dawn to the crow of a rooster. Except this rooster hailed from China, and his reveille competed with the wail of an Indian peacock, the screech of a Brazilian hyacinth macaw, and, if I was lucky, the laugh of an Australian kookaburra. Time to make my rounds. My charges would be expecting breakfast.

I crisscrossed a whole world of birds each day. In Australia I cleaned and sanitized bowls, hosed down floors, and prepared nectar and fruit for the lorikeets, singing out loud amidst their ceaseless chatter. After a few weeks I was amused to recognize echoes of my favorite Throwing Muses song in their repertoire.

In South America I chopped fruit in various sizes for various bird beaks, developing knife skills rivaling any prep cook. Larger chunks for the toucans, little nibbles for the cotingas. Boiled egg, peanuts, thawed mice, or horse meat for the omnivores or carnivores. Seeds for the finches. Parrot kibble for the parrots. Dozens of stainless-steel bowls lined the counters of the prep room where the radio was tuned to the modern rock sounds of 107.5 "The End." The Amazon Rainforest soundtrack in the background played louder as I swept and washed down inside floors and raked outside enclosures. Like maid service, except the guests never left and they watched me the whole time. I watched them too. Mutual voyeurism.

I didn't mind being watched by the birds, but the human visitors began to irk me. Once the aviary gates opened each day, I was on exhibit too. As I picked up discarded mouse parts and swept up turds, families pointed, laughed and chattered about the human in the kookaburra cage. Though only wire fences stood between us, they sometimes spoke about me as if I could not understand them. As if I were a bird too. "Maybe she can make the kookaburra laugh." Maybe I could. But I didn't.

I didn't know the natural history of many of my fellow residents but I did know their personal stories. Whether they'd been permanently injured in the wild or raised in captivity. Spending my days with them, I learned how they would react to me and how I should act around them to make them comfortable. I could recognize healthy, normal behavior and pick up on the subtle signs of stress or *dis-ease*. When you spend enough time around anybody, you learn the qualities and peculiarities that make each of us an individual.

I couldn't know how the birds felt about being in captivity, whether they even knew they were in captivity. In some, I recognized signs of contentment: the golden eagle who fell asleep on the glove in front of a rowdy bird show crowd and the East African crowned cranes who danced a perfectly synchronized mating ballet in the rectangle of their yard. To watch a snowy owl splash in a trough of ice water with obvious delight under the desert sun, to smile with pride as a mother black swan holds her head higher than usual with six newly hatched cygnets on her back, or to scratch the wingpits of a fuzzy-headed king vulture as he half shuts his eyes in total bliss is to understand that there are some things we all share.

I also recognized unrest. The sandhill crane who couldn't fly but managed to repeatedly jump up and flap out of his cage. The ground hornbill who paced tracks in the dirt and whacked her bill on the fence like a police baton on a jail cell anytime someone got too close. The Harris's hawk who flew at me with talons outstretched, scratching a bloody line down my face as I crumpled in the doorway, allowing him to escape. He perched in the cottonwoods above for days, finally coming down out of hunger, not knowing or remembering how to hunt for himself.

When I was not working as a barista or in the bird

buildings, chopping food or cleaning cages, I increasingly hid in my cabin and closed the shades so I couldn't see the throngs of people peering in my windows. But I could still hear them, could hear the children running after my peacocks, trying to catch their tail feathers or see if they could fly. I ached to run out there, screaming after the kids to see how they liked it. Captivity wore on me, too.

On the Fourth of July, the city staged fireworks in Liberty Park just outside the aviary grounds. Zoo staff had the best seats in town with no crowds, a small knoll inside the flamingo exhibit. I enjoyed a potluck dinner with my coworkers and then settled in for the show.

The lights were pretty but the noise was too loud, too close. My heart started beating too fast and I began to feel the old anxiety that sometimes snuck up on me when the human world was too loud, too much. Like a house or car alarm, an infant screaming or dog barking or my parents yelling at each other, that trapped-animal feeling that made me want to scream like a barn owl. Then I saw the flamingos.

Behind us, in the pond, seven Chilean flamingos stood in a circle with their heads underwater. I retreated to my cabin and got in bed. Under the covers.

Life in my gated community nurtured my introverted hermit tendencies. Though I occasionally enjoyed the big-city culture of live music, nightclub dancing, movies, cafes, and farmer's markets, I spent more time outside the city hiking the mountains alone or inside my fence, with the birds. The city overwhelmed me with people and noise everywhere, all the time. Why go out in that when next door a house full of parrots was just waiting to entertain?

The education parrots warbled their way into my heart. Intelligent and social like humans, they used the tools they had to make their desires known. Cleaning that building, I might witness a yellow-naped Amazon singing in his sweetest voice, "I left my heart in San Francisco" while swaying in time on his perch. Or an African gray might nod her head and inform me repeatedly "you're such a good bird, you're such a good bird" in a voice that sounded surprisingly like my own. The sulphur-crested cockatoo would raise her yellow crest and spread angelic wings for me to spritz with water, while she gurgled and squealed like a satisfied baby.

When the veterinarian came by to trim nails, file beaks, or give shots, these birds made their apprehension perfectly clear. The macaw who had been donated from a private owner because he was a biter screamed "Owwww!" The macaw who had been donated because he was a screamer yelled "Oh my god!" And the Amazon near the front door who regularly heard the instructions of the bird-show staff hollered "Shut the door!" And so it went, *Oww*, *Oh my god*, and *Shut the door* until the vet left them safely and securely alone in their barred cages.

None of us belonged in cages. The aviary was not my natural habitat any more than it was for Amazonian parrots or Chilean flamingoes. The difference was, I chose my captivity. Maybe I didn't experience all that my own culture had to offer in Salt Lake City. But from my brief immersion in bird culture, I do know why caged parrots sing, kookaburras laugh, flamingos hide, and banshees scream.

Catch and Release

Were flies always so loud? They were just regular house flies, as far as I could tell, though I'm not sure you still call them house flies when they are buzzing around a 9,000-foot peak in the Great Basin badlands of northeastern Nevada. Maybe they weren't loud so much as everything else was quiet. The harsh buzzy call of a Clark's nutcracker every now and then, the nasal chortle of a mountain chickadee, but otherwise, silence. No water noises – rivers or rain – because there was no water. No wind in the trees, because there were no leafy green trees. And conspicuously no people noise, because we were miles beyond and above the nearest potholed dirt road, and the twenty or so people on that mountain top with me were also sitting quietly, watching and listening, because that is what we were paid to do.

I blinked a few times to moisten my eyes in the arid heat, gave my recently shaved head a scratch, and then returned my hands to the string loop, my eyes scanning through the six-inch slit in the bird blind.

Out on the grey ridgetop ten yards ahead, my string threaded through an eyelet at the top of a pole, down to the leather harness on my lure bird – a pigeon – then over dust and rock back to the bird blind to complete the loop. Quickly but smoothly I pulled the right side of the string toward me, and released. The loop moved clockwise, the pigeon launched into the air and then released to flap back down to the ground. Pull, release: flap up, and down. Scan, and repeat, every few minutes.

The guy next to me on the wooden bench in the little shack controlled a European starling. The woman next to him, a house sparrow. Three invasive species trapped in the city, now living in a makeshift mountain aviary and working for us in the name of science. We were puppeteers orchestrating a raptor farce. When migrating birds of prey flew over the exposed ridge, they might dive in closer to see what the ruckus was about, and not be able to resist the temptation for a mid-migration snack. Birds that flap but don't go anywhere look like easy prey.

"Do you think those turkey vultures can smell us?" I wondered out loud, angling my vision up to the v-shaped silhouettes circling against the blue.

"I'm sure they smell me. I haven't showered in nine days," Liz said, giving her sparrow a tug. Flap flap flap, to stillness. Flies buzzed.

"I want an iced tea. With ice. That's the first thing I'm going to do the next time I go down," Rob mumbled.

"Mmmm, iced tea."

Flapping. Buzzing. Nothing. My eyes were droopy.

"When I die, I want to be up here, strung up to a bristlecone pine or left out for the cougars and vultures," Rob announced.

"Yeah," we agreed.

"Hey, we haven't gotten any golden eagles in a while. I want one so bad! Just one golden eagle, that's all I ask. Two more months." That was Liz.

"Yeah," we agreed.

Pull, release. Flapping.

That was pretty much the way it went in the trapping blind, most days, from sunup to sundown. Four other blinds perched on differently oriented ridges on that mountaintop held similar meaningful/meaningless conversations and a whole lot of quiet. Most of the time.

"Does anybody know what's for dinner? I hope it's not pasta aga..."

"INCOMING, TWO O'CLOCK!"

"It's a 'gos' going for the pigeon! Little flap now, Heather, don't scare him."

I sat up, rigid, arms electrified and fingers tingling. Tugged the string, released. The pigeon obeyed. A grey shadow was diving, getting closer.

"Good, now pull your pidge' in toward the bow net. Hold him. Coming in, get ready!"

A northern goshawk, the "grey ghost," the largest long-tailed short-winged accipiter, or forest hawk, landed next to my pigeon, closed his wings, and prepared to enjoy an easy meal.

"NOW!"

I yanked a different string to release the spring on the bow net, which sent the framed net over both birds' heads, trapping them.

"GO!"

I raced out of the blind toward the now shrieking, flapping tangle of birds, Liz behind me in case I needed help since I was the rookie. But I didn't need to think; my body acted, swiftly and correctly. Size up the situation – look for the dangerous part of the raptor, the talons. Use one hand to press the hawk gently to the ground so he doesn't hurt himself flapping, use the other to reach under the frame of the bow net to grab both legs. Open the net, tuck the bird's wing tips down into your hand so you hold him like an ice cream cone, the safest position for you both. Then trot to the rear of the blind to process your prize.

Liz checked the condition of the pigeon and found him physically unharmed under his leather armor. She smoothed his feathers, re-set the bow net, and followed me to the shade behind the blind to our little bird cage, where she chose another pigeon to switch out with mine. He deserved a rest, some food and water, and it was nearly the end of his two-hour shift anyway. We didn't pretend it was a happy life for the lure birds, but we tried to keep it from being too terrible. We were all bird-lovers, after all, though many of us were a little prejudiced toward the regal raptors.

A lizard scuttled out from behind the pile of differently sized cans as I chose one, coffee-can sized, to place over the goshawk's head. Big can for this species – a female, probably. Males are always smaller. Supported in the dark, she calmed immediately, her muscled legs quieting and relaxing in my hands. I remained attentive to her feet, which if I let free could easily seize and pierce deeply into my hand then grip tightly, effortlessly, like a vice.

I cradled the head-in-a-can end of the bird in the crook of my elbow and balanced her weight on my lap as I started the measurements and made notes on my clipboard. I knew she was an adult, as she had the light grey body and crimson eyes of a mature goshawk rather than the streaky brown body and yellow or orange eyes of a juvenile. This bird had been around a few years, had made this migration before. The bulge in her throat, her crop, suggested she'd eaten recently, and the fat deposits along her breastbone and in her wingpits told me she was healthy. Other measurements meant less to me there, in the field, but were part of a pool of data that together can track the health and trends of raptor populations.

I had less than ten minutes with her. Five if I was speedy,

which I aimed to be so I could send her on her way with minimal stress. The final step was a uniquely numbered silver band I closed gently around her ankle. After making sure it fit as it should, loose and mobile on her leg but not so bulky it would catch on anything, I readied myself for release.

Standing and firming my grip around wing tips and legs, I stepped back into the sunlight. I slowly pulled the can off her and her head whipped around to face me. We were eye to eye. Squinting blue eyes, sunburned and freckled skin, wide smile. Unblinking red eyes, feathers the color of pewter streaked with ash, mouth open, silent. We locked together. We connected.

I knew why we did the research. Furthermore, I had learned how to effectively communicate the why to school field trips and scout groups, families and lone hikers, any who were willing to drive one hour south from the nearest Nevada town or three hours across the Great Salt Lake Desert from Salt Lake City, brave the three-mile hike straight up this Goshute Mountain peak in the high desert to check out the largest hawk migration site in the western United States. Which was a surprisingly high number of people.

As one of HawkWatch International's educators, I explained the importance of predatory animals as indicators of the health of ecosystems, our goal to follow trends in population size and health in order to recognize problems while there is still time to address them. That was the public face of our research, the big why.

But why was I up there? Why did I shave my head to live in a tent on a shower-less desert mountain for three months? I believed in the big why; of course I did. But I believed in other things, too. The long days of silence, flies buzzing, ravens calling, and quail families tottering about under prickly rabbitbrush. I believed in sleeping on hard ground in a tent village, listening to poorwills cooing and coyotes wailing. And in pulling on winter boots and stepping out of my tent at 3 a.m. to pee, to find a foot of pristine October snow glistening beneath more stars than I thought possible to see with the naked eye.

There was beauty, yes, but there was also a simplicity in the life that I'd yearned for, that made all the noise and busy-ness down below seem absurd. This was what I knew in theory when I signed up to rough it on a mountaintop for less than minimum wage. This was what I understood with all my senses at the first morning meeting, eating oatmeal and drinking tea from a tin cup as the sun turned the Great Salt Lake Desert below neon orange. Even if I never caught a single bird, even if I didn't get to sink my fingertips deep in the feathers of a prairie falcon or feel the nip of a kestrel on a knuckle, I would believe in the experience simply for the way I got to live, for a while. Life in the Goshutes just seemed more real, more true. Human drama – what was the point of that again? I was above it. Nine thousand feet above it.

That goshawk in my hands, she was the cream on top. When a hot wind gusted over us, she freed her wingtips from my grip and opened them slightly, still holding my gaze. Liz snapped a picture. Then, in one swift move I raised my arm and opened my hand. She flapped once, twice, rising vertically, shook out all her feathers as if putting the whole bewildering business behind her and then glided away. As she circled, her new silver band flashed in the sunlight and then the grey ghost was gone, following the ridgeline south toward her wintering grounds. She left me in the dust, on the earth where I belong.

No time for wistfulness; there was work to do. Back in the blind, I shifted to position on the sparrow. Flap flap flap. Buzz. Quiet.

"Nice gos, Heather."

"Thanks, Rob."

The starling flapped.

"Hey next time we hit a bad weather stretch, we're going down to the hot springs out in that canyon outside of Wells. It's unmarked but Bob knows how to get there. You in?"

"Definitely."

We often talked about what we would do when we came down from the mountain during rare days off or when the weather was too bad for birds to fly, but nobody brought up the time after the field season ended. This was taboo, and we all subconsciously knew better. Some were headed to jobs at ski resorts, others to winter semester of college, a lucky few south to another field research position, but many would be unemployed and couch-surfing until the next seasonal gig rolled around.

I didn't know, myself, and normally that would worry me. It should have worried me. But it was hard to think of life off of the mountain, to even remember it was still going on without me. It hurt my brain; the reality was so distinct. And so I remained there, staring out at silvery-green sagebrush, darker green twigs of Mormon tea, and a few scattered bristlecone pines. I remained there listening to the nutcrackers and chickadees. Sometimes you really can *be here now*. Sometimes you can't help it.

If I sent my awareness anywhere else, it was with the birds we watched, the birds we trapped, banded, and released. I wondered where they were headed, where they would land. Especially a certain bird with red eyes I wouldn't be able to get out of my head for quite some time. I can still feel her gaze on me.

One of the studies I remember best from my college psychology classes involved strangers paired up and made to stare intently into one another's eyes. They did not speak nor were they allowed to meet up outside the study. Many of them reported developing feelings of love toward the objects of their gaze. I recall some of them formed romantic relationships afterward, though I haven't been able to find confirmation of that.

Neurobiologists have taught us that in the right conditions, eye contact stimulates release of phenylethylamine, a neurotransmitter that stimulates other neurotransmitters like dopamine and serotonin to evoke feelings of exhilaration, elation, and attraction. Romantic love. If we humans stare long enough at anything with the ability to stare back, deep connections are made, regardless of the words we use to explain them. Maybe even regardless of the return gaze.

I don't pretend that the goshawk felt anything like love for me. Logically I know she was probably experiencing her own flurry of chemicals more in line with fear and stress. But that isn't what I felt. I felt part of something good, something true.

Those three months as a raptor researcher I spent a lot of time staring deeply. At birds, at trees, at lizards, grasshoppers, the dusty dirt. Whether they stared back or not, I felt something for each of them.

And what of human connection? Liz, Rob, and the rest of my little community? We spent intimate hours side by side in trapping blinds or at the observation lookout, evenings huddled by the fire, singing hippie folk songs and drinking hot chocolate with peppermint schnapps. Treks to valley hot springs where we'd lounge naked and steaming in the rain and then crowd six people to a motel room to save money. It was a fun, easy togetherness, but were there deeper connections there? Eyes met, phenylethylamine released? Not from me. No. Honestly, I remember the look of the bristlecone pine trees more clearly than the faces of my crewmembers.

So. Was I hiding from reality, on the outside looking in? Or, was I living my reality, on the outside looking out?

I do know this. At 9,000 feet above sea level, where the air was thin and the sky stretched out forever, where sagebrush was more intoxicating than roses could ever be, I fell in love with a red-eyed bird, and I let her go.

C Is for Cat

Alligators

What you notice first are the alligators on the side of the road. You aren't sure how you feel about alligators, but figure you better accept them since you came here to help rehabilitate wildlife and it doesn't get much wilder than a seven-hundred-pound dinosaur cousin with spiked body armor and a toothy grin. Welcome to Florida.

Boobies

Alligators are hardly the strangest wildlife found in south Florida. What exactly is a manatee? Aren't armadillos supposed to live in the desert? That lanky swimming snake with wings is an anhinga. Forget flamingos; check out the roseate spoonbills. Or mangrove cuckoos, magnificent frigatebirds, and if you're lucky, two species of boobies.

Cages

The inside cages are for the very small, like orphaned mockingbirds, or the very sick, like the bobcat with a head trauma. Outside cages are for animals closer to release, like the gopher tortoise healing a cracked shell. There are flight cages for the birds and enclosures big enough for bears to run and bobcats to leap. The in-ground pool hosts a lively party attended by a motley assortment of cormorants, terns, anhingas, and pelicans.

Death

You see animals die from collisions with cars, cat attacks, fishing line and six-pack holders encircling beaks or necks, fish hook impalement, parasites, poison, dehydration, bullet wounds, and unknown causes. The worst is electrocution, which cooks an animal from the inside out. You slice open a recently dead osprey to find his organs well-done.

You hold a coyote still while the veterinarian administers a lethal injection. Under bright lights you stroke her fur as if you are a comfort. As if she was your pet dog. She is warm under your hands long after she closes her eyes.

When the vet isn't onsite you use the gas chamber – an airtight box attached to a canister of carbon dioxide. They only struggle for a few seconds. Once they are still, you bag them and put them in the freezer for later incineration.

Empathy

Charismatic megafauna are your favorites. Bears, deer, coyotes, bobcats. It's basic human psychology to prefer animals more closely related to and resembling ourselves.

Fish Mix

You chop fruits and vegetables, pour kibble and seeds, prepare bottles for the babies. Thaw fish, chickens, mice and rats for the carnivores. Tube feed the animals who cannot or will not eat on their own: one person holding the mouth open and another inserting a thin tube down the throat to the stomach and pumping in a carefully measured amount of liquefied food. For sea birds, you blend fish and vitamin oil in the most repulsive concoction you've ever smelled. It smells the same when pelicans throw it back up on you.

Gannets

These large white booby-cousins spend most of their lives at sea. Except for the one that washes up on a local beach, weak and malnourished, spends a month in the clinic fattening up on fish mix, gets released, and washes up on the same beach one month later.

Herons, Eagles, and Other Pick-Ups

You stalk an eagle tangled in fishing line who manages to stay just beyond reach in a mangrove thicket. You play tag with a great blue heron with a broken wing who can still outrun you. In your blue Conservancy of Southwest Florida polo shirt and protective eye goggles, you chase him up and down the dunes until finally throwing a towel over him and tackling him to the ground. You are just. Trying. To save. His life. Goddammit.

Incarceration

The act of confining what would otherwise be free. Captivity.

Justification

People just want to help. You see the relief in their faces when they hand over their charges – the sick, the injured, the huddled masses rescued from certain death.

You just want to help, too. But after you wrap the bandages, pump food down their throats, and lock them in cages, what you feel is nothing like relief.

Kites

Three swallow-tailed kites with bumblefoot have been in the clinic for over a year. They came in weak and malnourished, but by the time they were rehabilitated they'd missed their migration south to Brazil for the winter. When spring rolled around, they'd all developed the bacterial infection common to captive birds of prey with inadequate perches, so they have to stay in the inside cages. Every other day you clean, ointment, and re-bandage their feet. They are calm and make little chirping noises now and then. You wonder whether they remember what outside feels like. You wonder if they will ever leave.

Laundry

There are towels in all the cages, towels used to capture and restrain animals, towels to wrap the dead ones, to mop up regurgitated fish mix. Towels soiled with blood and poop and fish scales. You do several loads of laundry per day, all towels, so for years the smell of Arm & Hammer powder detergent on a towel will make you feel like you better get a move on and start feeding or cleaning something.

Motherhood

Baby mammals who are soft and warm and who reach for you with little hands awaken a maternal instinct you never knew you had. Raccoons quickly become your favorites. Whenever you come through the door, three cooing, crying orphans tug at your ankles with cool fingers. They fidget and fuss when you bottle feed them, except when you hold the bottle in one hand and scratch their backs with the other, wherein they snuggle into your lap and purr like contented kittens.

Needles

You learn to draw up saline for dehydration, dexamethasone for head injuries, and sulfa drugs for infections. Measure in cc's and tap the syringe to get the air bubbles out, just like a doctor. Or a heroin addict. Either way, you feel like a badass.

Opossums

Baby opossums look like little fetuses, which they pretty much are since they are supposed to finish developing in their mother's pouch. But sometimes moms get hit by cars and kindhearted folks bring in the babies. They have wrinkly pink skin and toothy grimaces only a mother could love, aside from you apparently, since you sort of want to take them home in your pockets. Their little hands are like Velcro to hold on to Mom, which comes in handy at feeding time. In a cage of six identical opossum babies, for example, you can pull them all out and hang them on your shirt. Then just pry one off, feed it, and put it back in the cage.

Prey

A woman brings in a duck she rescued from an alligator. You don't have the heart to ask her, *but what about the alligator?*

Questions

When an animal has ten babies each year, aren't some of them supposed to die? When wild animals are weak, sick, or injured, how do we affect evolution when we fix them and put them back? Are we messing with nature, or have we already done so much harm that we are offsetting that by doing some good? Does the stress of captivity have lasting effects?

Are you here just because you want to touch wild animals?

Release

Take a boat ride into turquoise Gulf waters and open the kennel. Watch the gannet waddle out, pose on the bow, look around for a few seconds, then belly flop into the sea, wiggling his tail feathers.

Drive to a wildlife sanctuary and release the adolescent raccoons who keep running back to you at first but eventually toddle off into the jungle.

Stand with your fellow interns in the Big Cypress Preserve, each holding a swallow-tailed kite in your arms. Together, give them a gentle toss up into the sky and pray that they fly. They all do.

Scars

The divot where the pelican grabbed your forearm instead of the fish. The "V" on your inner thigh when you didn't hold the loon's head firmly enough while tube-feeding him and he whipped around and grabbed you. The smaller "v" on the webbing between thumb and forefinger where the tern latched on and shook your hand like a sardine.

Time

You feed, you clean, you chase, you fold towels, you feed again, then let them go or hold them while they die. Fall into bed, exhausted. Repeat. No time to process the rollercoaster ride you're on. It comes at you in compact fragments like film strips. Though a typical day might involve administering a shot to a baby alligator, throwing a chicken to a bobcat, wearing nine opossums, and chatting with the pelican perched on a chair in the kitchen while his cage is being cleaned, you are too busy moving from one thing to another to marvel at your current existence.

Unlocked

Twice, someone leaves the bobcat cage unlocked. The first time, she stays in her cage. The second time, you find her sitting on a windowsill, watching the birds outside. *The cat is out*, you say to the others, unblinking, and someone throws a chicken in the cage so she'll go back in. She does.

Veterinarian

You never wanted to be a traditional veterinarian but always thought you might want to get into wildlife rehabilitation. Now you aren't so sure.

Wild

"A weasel is wild. Who knows what he thinks?"
–Annie Dillard

X-rays

You order x-rays and take fecal samples, bandage wounds and give shots, but you will never really know if you are helping.

Domesticated animals are motivated to make their desires known. Wild animals are not. They can't tell you if they'd rather die in the swamp or be food for an alligator, that they really are fine and their parents are coming back for them or that they agree that fish mix is disgusting.

Yowl

The cat is in an outside enclosure now, nearing time for release. She seems a different animal than the docile feline on the windowsill. When you go out to throw her a chicken she crouches with haunches in the air, bares her teeth and hisses. Wiggles her rear, lowers her head, locks eyes with you and yowls. You open the cage just enough to throw in dinner and slam it shut again. You remember to lock it.

Zenith

At the end of your six months you hand over your key, pack up your station wagon, and drive away from a purple sunset over the Gulf of Mexico, threading your way north. Alligators line the roadway, inert.

Pinacate

At the base of a brick-red basalt boulder on the coal-black lava field, something shone white in the Sonoran sunshine. Blinding white, too white even for my sunglass-protected eyes, so that the backs of my eyeballs began to throb as I stared and stared.

I smiled. Then whispered, *Hola.*

Silence. I turned to look behind me, then scanned the desert all around. The avocado green of stately saguaro, wiry ocotillo, and squat, furry looking teddy-bear cholla scattered atop tar-colored volcanic rock gave the landscape the feel of an unkempt vacant lot. In the distance inky cinder cones and crater edges shimmered in the heat waves.

I drew in a hot breath and licked my lips.

All was still and quiet. Not library quiet, not doctor's office quiet, nor even the quiet of my Rocky Mountain foothills home, but white noise quiet, like wearing earmuffs.

I was alone, four hours and a zigzag line away from

basecamp where I would meet fellow desert ecology students by sundown. It was the middle of a two-week field trip through Baja and Sonora, and it was solo day. That morning our group of twelve scattered to the four directions and I hadn't seen so much as another human footprint since. If I closed my eyes, I could disappear too.

I held my breath and was gone.

Eyes open. Exhale. Empty eye sockets stared back at me from below the base of curved white horns.

That morning, over oatmeal, one of our teachers told us of a bighorn sheep skull he found somewhere in this desert a couple years ago. Tugging at his beard, eyes twinkling, he dared us. *Someone should find it again.*

I scanned the ground for stray cacti spines, wiped away a few of the sharper-looking pebbles, and sat cross-legged in front of the skull. Gathering the chalk-pale bones delicately onto my lap, I traced the arc of the horns from forehead to tips, then back down a long snout to the hole where a nose would be. Resting on my shins were the jagged upper jaw teeth, not quite as sharp as the points of scoria basalt digging into my hips below me. I took the skull in my hands again, brought it up to face me, and then knocked it lightly onto my sun-baked and freckled forehead. *Ow.* Bighorn sheep were made for that; I was decidedly not.

Deserts breed hardness, sharpness, roughness. That desert more than most. They say the substrate of Sonora's Pinacate desert is closest on earth to that of the moon. In every direction under cobalt sky a crumbled opaque charcoal, like weathered asphalt, sparsely speckled with the smooth oily shine of volcanic glass.

Though I was posing as a mountain dweller up north in Colorado, I am from the soft, lush, verdant hills of New England. My ancestors are from the similar terrain and moody mists of northern Europe. I feared I was unfit for the desert landscape. Too fragile. Too pale. Too soft. Everything around me highlighted my weaknesses. I didn't belong there.

I settled my gaze on the darkness of the ground next to me, resting my eyes from the glaring white sheep skull. A speckle of smooth shiny midnight began to move. Steadily, marching just above the ground, any shadow swallowed by the black earth. No animated volcanic glass, no heatstroke hallucination, it was a pinacate beetle, from the Aztec, *pinacatl*. Black desert named for black beetle. Darkling beetle moonscape.

I closed my eyes again and pictured my northern home. Right then, in March at 8,000 feet, fresh snow frosted the packed drifts. Everything frozen, everywhere white. My mountain cabin was dark, my bed empty. There I was learning to live on my own again, remembering how to feel whole instead of half of two. Trying to forgive someone who lied to me, wounded me, and to forgive myself for letting it happen again and again. A different sort of desert, with a different sort of roughness.

Eyes open, back to my moonscape.

How fortunate to get to explore that foreignness the way I was, the way we were. A group of graduate students, professors, and alumni thrown together on a blue-painted school bus rumbling through northern Mexico. We hiked by day and spent the night camping on parched earth under arid skies.

Most days were full of excited chatter, laughter, and song, the sounds of shared adventure. Such experiences make people feel close quickly. Campfires breed intimacy. We shared secrets and promised to keep in touch once the trip ended. I reveled in the togetherness, even knowing, at a jaded thirty-three, that it would fade quickly once we returned to our faraway homes.

That day it felt good to stand on my own, fragile as I was. I gulped from my water bottle and pulled my hat lower on my forehead. I slathered on another layer of sunscreen and tucked the bottle back into my backpack. Standing, I placed the skull on the red basalt and stretched my legs. A hot breeze lifted my arm hairs and a few strands of yellowed grass under a palo verde tree nearby. Black grains blew against my bare legs. I was eroding already.

I crunched four steps toward the palo verde, a sprawling, smooth, green-skinned grandmother of a tree. I intended to rest in her shade but by the look of the ground I knew I'd have to stick to the edge. The mess of cholla spines carpeting the pebbles around a round hole were likely signs of a wood rat burrow entrance. Barbed wire fortress. There are no welcome mats in the desert.

The desert is not spiteful or cruel. Desert flora grows rough and spiny just to survive the climate and keep from being eaten by every water-seeking creature. Desert animals require the same protections. The wood rats underneath me drinking cactus juice in their thorn-protected burrow didn't know any different.

I think I might like to grow thorns. Sharp spines that barb anyone who grabs at me, tries to take from me, moves toward me any way other than delicately. Or thick boney horns I can point in front of me to shield the soft, sensitive parts. Not cruel, protected.

The afternoon light had shifted, and I looked up on the slant of the cinder cone ahead to see a faint line along the hillside. There was a recessed trail in the cinders. We'd learned about that. It was one of the paths of the indigenous Tohono O'odham, the desert people. Strong enough for the Pinacate, they did belong there. Their journeys preserved in the arid dust. To follow the paths of the Tohono O'odham was to find water, or the memory of water.

Memories of water, memories of a people, memories of a furred horned mammal. Memories of a whole. The sere desert mummifies them all. But there were more than memories there.

The wood rat. The beetle. The palo verde, saguaro, and cholla all there, then. As I was there. And though I may be softer, paler, more fragile than the Tohono O'odham, I too was finding my own way in the desert.

The slant of light told me it was time to retrace my tracks and return to camp. We would all have stories to share by the campfire. I had one. I turned back to the skull where I left it on the red rock, and whispered, *Gracias.*

Feral

The woman opened the cardboard kennel and the cat hopped out onto the burgundy rug and started grooming. Rear paws pointed at the ceiling, claws extended, the cat smoothed the caramel fur of her belly with her sandpaper tongue. She didn't know where she was, only that it was better than the cage of metal and stone where she'd been locked for a year. This room built of tree trunks held fuzzy blankets on soft chairs, sun-warmed wood floors and bookshelves, and no sign of other cats or nasty old dogs. The woman sitting cross-legged in front of her smiled with her mouth, though her eyes were glazed and her fingers pulled at her throat as though encumbered by her own skin.

Instead of exhaust, pavement, and street rats, the cat smelled trees, moving water, and rocky earth. Large panes of glass revealed a yellow world. Green-yellow, lemon-yellow, and orange-yellow leaves pinwheeled on the wind, frosted toothy boulders, and summersaulted through a creek. Above the yellow, legions of needled pines posed against white pyramids pointing at the bluebird sky.

The woman found the place behind the cat's ears that made her purr, sighed and said, *Welcome to the Rocky Mountains, new friend. It's just you and me, now.* She'd planned to keep this cat inside, to keep her safe from cougars, coyotes, and cars, but as she watched the animal survey the rocky ridges of her home, eyes dancing over the landscape, the woman recognized the same glint in those green eyes as in her own blue ones. The need that will not be contained.

One bright day in a string of bright days they padded up the path together, alert, looking in all directions, gulping the montane air. Step step step pause, look, sniff, step step step. When a loudmouth jay announced the cat's presence the woman whispered *Sorry, jay—you better get used to her. She's with me.*

That Colorado autumn, they were busy. Cat needed to zip up an aspen tree, sink her claws into the powdery white bark, and hang there for long seconds before shimmying back down and attacking another. Woman needed to squat on her haunches and pick stones from the icy creek, and to tilt her head and listen to sounds beneath the trickling brook, beyond the rustling aspens. They both needed to scrutinize the mountain chickadees and nuthatches fluttering and tinkling in the ponderosas.

While the cat stalked the yellows tumbling in the wind, the woman lay on her stomach on warm rock and peered at the thread-thin decaying ones. Looked so closely she could see gold and silver fibers sparkling in the sun, and murmured, *Are we all iridescent, up close?*

Often, the woman needed to cry.

About the place she'd left, the woman she'd left behind. Years of commitment, nesting, wedding plans, life plans. Real love. But love looked her in the eye and lied. Love snuck away to a mutual friend's bed. The woman who was supposed to be The One said, *Trust me, it won't happen again.* But it did, over and over. The woman who was supposed to be different from a man, who was supposed to be tender, honest, and true, wasn't.

Those fragile places where love and trust lie deep in the body, places already damaged by parents who were supposed to be in love but who shouted and hurt one another, over and over, those places shattered.

Broken, her body fell ill and her voice disappeared. For five weeks she was diminished to whispers, when all she wanted was to scream.

When the woman woke from her nightmares, twitching and whimpering, the cat snuggled in, purring. The woman did the same for the cat, stroking away her bad memories of life before.

Sometimes they looked in the mirror. Black diamond pupils, charcoal stripes on ashen fur. Midnight-black hair, furrowed blond eyebrows, scarred cheeks from when her dog sunk his jaws into her, further shredding trust.

Who am I? she said. *Meow?* she said.

Rocky Mountain winters last many moons and are best spent hibernating. Not the deathly sleep of bats and mice, but the lazy torpor of bears. And cats. Rosemary olive-oiled root vegetables sizzling in the oven, baroque music on the radio, they snuggled and snoozed the days away. Cat followed sunbeams across the walls, through the crystals rainbowing down on the desk, bed, and rug, her whiskers and tail twitching with the effort of not pouncing on each one. Woman devoured books that made her nod and smile with her whole face. *Gary Snyder, Kathleen Dean Moore, Barry Lopez. Barbara Kingsolver, Kim Stafford, Ana Maria Spagna...*

Outside the snow hissed, and yowling winds tossed pine boughs against the crystalline sky but it couldn't touch them in there. They both slept more soundly, then.

Sometimes when the wind stopped, in between snows,

they tried walking outside. The cat tiptoed on top of the soft cold but the woman grunted, snorted and laugh-growled as she sunk up to her waist. The creek was gone then, buried with the leaves of fall under all that white and quiet. Before long, they retreated to the comfort of inside, back to their den, where they stared out the porthole into the twilight ocean where they didn't belong, not in winter. It was the time to sleep, and wait.

One day the woman brought a stranger home with her. They had frenetic sex on the bed while the cat watched. Afterward the woman cried so hard she couldn't breathe and the stranger left soon after.

That was a bad idea. We are solitary animals.

Hibernation resumed. Wind blew. Snow drifted. The woman shoveled the path to her car, unburied it and returned to clear the drifts from the windows so they could see out. The next day she did it again. They ate a lot, and slept. Rocky Mountain winters last many moons.

But spring always comes. Finally, sweet stormy air seeped through the windows blowing ponderosa kisses. Sleet flicked the tin chimney top and shushed the snow off the roof into the melting creek. Everything was waking up, they were waking up, inhaling the breath of a new year.

The woman liked the thunderstorms. They watched them slide across the plains, silvery orange and gold light whisking cloud shadows across the sky. They waited in the charged air, soundless, for the rumbling rains to come. Stood in the open door, tasting the air with their tongues.

One morning when violet-green swallows fanned the sky like peacock feathers, the cat sniffed something new on the air. Familiar, but wilder than she. Picking her way toward the woodland she saw him, stalking squirrels at the bird feeder. She couldn't help herself, snuck up behind him and startled him, chased him up a tree. The woman heard the growling, came out and looked from small cat, dainty paws hugging the base of the spruce tree, up to bigger cat, meaty paws gripping the first branch ten feet up. He was easily three times her size, spotted and nubby-tailed. Bobcat.

Cat. Bobcat. Woman.

The woman spoke.

Jade, no!

Bobcat leaped down and ran. Cat chased bobcat. Woman chased cat. They all sprinted through slushy snow, on decomposing leaves and needles, along the thundering snowmelt creek and over boulders, up the ridge toward the mountains.

Bobcat was too fast, too far ahead gone up the mountain, so the cat stopped. The game was over. The woman scooped her up, brought her back toward the house. At the wooden footbridge over the creek they flopped down together, breathing hard. *You're crazy,* she said, and they squint-smiled at each other and the cat purred. The woman flipped onto her back with arms slack behind her head. Watched the branches, the clouds, the sky. Her face was softening, her insides thawing too.

The snow continued to melt and spring sprung in all its luxurious flamboyance. The cat raced up trees again. The woman sat on a rock, her back against a ponderosa, a throne of stone and root. They listened to ravens and watched spiders and fuzzy orange beetles. Crickets violined and songbirds multiplied at the feeder. Lizards and snakes came out to sun with them.

The poison was going from her, the broken parts healing. Not healing like new, but rougher, like scar tissue. Like the Rocky Mountains. She was a little less like her kind, a little more like the cat. And both of them were a little more like bobcat.

One grey misty day, the kind that only happened a few times a year in those parts, the woman started to write. She wrote of cedar trees and salmon rivers that flow to the ocean. Of moss- and fern-carpeted rain forests where snow never buries creeks and birds sing all winter long. A warmer, gentler place that would take them in like the Rocky Mountains had, but maybe soften the rough edges.

She came back from town with different hair, the black dye shaved off, gold and silver stubble shining in the sun. And new ink on her skin – a red and black fish over a blue river. *A symbol of the Pacific Northwest. A salmon to lead us home.*

Before the forest turned yellow again, woman tucked cat into a Penske truck and drove to where the mist meets the river and the river meets the sea. *No aspens*, she said, *but you're going to love the cottonwoods.*

Paradise Prison

"It's me that's changed and done all this and come and gone and complained and hurt and joyed and yelled, not the Void."

—Jack Kerouac

In Washington State's rugged North Cascades mountains, there is a narrow valley carved by an ancient glacier and sculpted by the Skagit River, a valley just wide enough to contain stream-fed Diablo Lake, a pot-holed road at its edge, and the campus of North Cascades Institute. This was my paradise.

"You ready for the commute?" my new coworker Manda winked, pointing out the bay window of the staff house, where a narrow path disappeared behind six-foot snowdrifts and frosted firs.

"Bring it on!" I said, excited for my first day of seasonal work as a 'spring' naturalist. "I'll be outside."

Stepping out into the snow I promptly sank up to my

thighs. Chuckling, I plodded to the packed path and waited for seasoned employees Manda and Kevin.

So this was March in the North Cascades. I breathed the dry cold, enjoying the sensation of my nose hairs freezing and thawing with each inhale and exhale.

I listened to the quiet. It was a stillness so complete that I was sure I could hear individual snowflakes falling, a quiet so all-encompassing that when pierced by a raven's bell-like call note I jumped and looked around, sure the bird was right above me. But there was nothing but a white sky and the wintry calm. My new friends appeared and we turned to go.

They led me up – in such a landscape there is always up – a well-trodden switchbacked path to the top of a ridge, through a stand of lodgepole pines and out onto an unplowed service road. Looming ahead was a colossal concrete wall holding back a mountain of water. Kevin, a dam enthusiast with the speed-talking late-for-work energy of a northeasterner, gave me my first lesson in the history of my new home.

He spread his arms wide and exclaimed, "This is Diablo Dam. This three-hundred-eighty-nine-foot-tall dam and the five-hundred-foot-tall Ross Dam at the other end transformed what was formerly a section of the Skagit river into Diablo Lake. These and a third dam downriver comprise the Skagit River Hydroelectric Project, which supplies Seattle with almost twenty percent of its power. In your job you will be leading dam walks and giving dam tours, so you will get to know more dam facts than you ever wanted. Any dam questions?"

It was going to be a fun year.

We crunched snowy tracks along the main road around the lake toward the institute's office, my soon-to-be coworkers and friends, and my new life. I craned my neck up at the aptly named Pyramid Peak where the sun that hadn't yet reached us shone brightly. I was jubilant. There was nowhere else I would rather be than that road less-traveled. Just me, my friendly little community, the ravens, and the quiet.

It is difficult to describe the North Cascades without using words like pristine, majestic, or splendor. Like a movie backdrop, the landscape is almost implausibly picturesque. Jagged snowy peaks rise nearly vertically, giving the range the nickname "The American Alps." These are not a handful of cone-shaped volcanic peaks perched in wide valleys like the central and southern Cascades. This is a crowded rocky tapestry with names right out of a Tolkien book: Prophet, Desolation, Triumph, Despair.

This uplifted mountain range hosts the most active glaciers in North America outside of Alaska, far more than Glacier National Park. The icy blue behemoths continue to carve the landscape and feed lakes like Diablo, turning it eerie green with flour-fine glacial silt. An aerial photograph of 1,200-foot Diablo Lake cradled in the arms of 7,200-foot Pyramid Peak, 6,000-foot Sourdough Mountain, and 7,400-foot Ruby is more reminiscent of Alaskan backcountry than a Seattle daytrip.

That's what I thought when I first researched the area. Where I grew up on the East Coast, mountains are gentler, worn and crumbling. I'd lived in some wild places, from the Florida Everglades to the Colorado Rockies, the Utah red rock desert to western Oregon's river valleys, but something about the severity and remoteness of the least-visited national park was particularly enticing.

Or maybe it was just time to move on again. There is a condition in migratory animals known as "zugunruhe," a chemical and behavioral migratory restlessness. The longing that starts as mild agitation and progresses through unrest to anxious panic. The desire to be gone that becomes impossible to ignore.

I'd only been in Portland, Oregon for six months, but when I got the job offer with North Cascades Institute I jumped at the opportunity to leave the tame city for a new adventure in wild America. I packed up everything that would fit in my VW Jetta, gave away the rest, then hit the road north toward my new paradise.

The North Cascades were everything but tame, and as the snow melted my wild community grew. A golden-eyed bobcat crouched on the scree slope above the entrance road. Screeching peregrine falcons nested on the ridge above the staff house. A slinky brown pine marten nosed around the compost building looking for scraps, and cougar tracks traced an intimate path around the office and between the dorms.

And bears! Once the land greened up and huckleberries ripened, black bears were suddenly everywhere. One bear camped out for a week not one hundred yards from the staff house, sprawled in the ferns like a stuffed animal, snapping at flies. Another bear lumbered boldly down the dirt path through campus while ecstatic school kids watched from their dorms.

"Hey, um, Heather? There's a bear," a middle schooler stammered, pointing at a bear plodding across the trail just uphill from where we had paused on our hike, taking a water break. The bear ignored us, heading for the lake and a water break of his own. Bountiful bears.

Paradise wasn't all in the noteworthy, call your city friends and boast experiences. It was also in the more humble moments of the chaotic three-ring circus of teaching children freed from classrooms. In the group of eleven-year-olds who forgot themselves and joined me stalking through tall grass on hands and knees toward a deer to see how close we could get, then squealing with delight at the deer's surprised look before it sprang away. The spark of understanding visible in the student who suddenly fathomed that where we stood had once been buried a mile-deep in ice, the way she looked with new eyes at the topography around her. And the weekly closing campfires where, steeped in sweet cedar smoke, each child made a wish for the earth, spoke it out loud, and then threw a cedar sprig into the snapping sparking fire.

"I hope when I grow up the North Cascades is still here, just like this, so I can come back and be a teacher here."

I hoped so too.

In summer, as we bade farewell to school groups and welcomed family and adult programs, the landscape completed its transformation from Ansel Adams' stark beauty to vivid showy Monet. The palette boasted a complete color wheel from red crossbill to purple lupine. The most surreal color swirled into Diablo Lake. What was in winter a stormy ocean blue became an almost radioactive neon turquoise.

On my knees in a wooden canoe, I dipped my paddle in time with a buddy and we headed out to the middle of this fantasy world. *Dip, pull, glide... dip, pull, glide...* on the sparkly green deep. The peaks stood tall all around us, still snow-kissed and gusting icy reminders that winter remained up there. Below us the expansive glacial puddle would never warm enough for a comfortable swim. But there on the surface of our valley, with the sun on our faces, we drank in summer's blessings. The breeze frosting the water into whitecaps whispered, *You belong.*

One morning that summer, as a special treat, the staff piled into vans and drove higher into the mountains to find true alpine meadows. Up there amidst my namesake, *Phyllodoce empetriformis* – wild mountain heather – we were handed butterfly nets. We scampered through the fields, pouncing and missing more than we caught. When we did discover captives in our nets, we were taught how to carefully remove the butterflies to keep from crushing them and how to hold them safely while we identified them.

When we were ready to release them our director and

butterfly enthusiast, Saul, gathered us around him and looked out for a moment at the field of lilies and heather. Then he whispered, as if sharing a secret, "Butterflies get cold when still, like snakes in the shade, so they have to warm in the sun before flying. If we give them a comfortable place to rest and warm up, they might stick around for a while."

Then he took the large yellow and black tiger swallowtail he'd been holding and lowered it onto my forehead. I stood alert and barely breathing as six tiny feet touched down on my skin and wings brushed each eyebrow. For twenty minutes I beamed brighter than the sun with my butterfly halo, until it flapped once, twice, then rose into the cloudless sky. I couldn't imagine heaven gets any better.

~

In Washington state's rugged North Cascades mountains, there is a narrow valley carved by an ancient glacier and sculpted by the Skagit River, a valley just wide enough to contain stream-fed Diablo Lake, the pot-holed road at its edge, and the campus of North Cascades Institute. This was my prison.

In the early fall I had joyfully accepted a permanent position with the institute, but by winter's return, paradise was nowhere to be found. Something else had creeped into me, so slowly that I didn't recognize its presence until it was undeniably there.

One afternoon as Manda and I trudged through unplowed snow along the road to the dam, it struck me that the Skagit River is trapped between concrete walls. Stagnant, doomed to stillness. I gazed up at the granite walls bearing down on me, feeling an agitated longing hovering on anxious panic, as if I was entombed with the dismembered river. I nudged Manda, pointed up toward Pyramid Peak, and said, "Look, the sun is setting." It was 1 p.m.

The gusty wind made it difficult to stand upright out on the dam, but we braced ourselves and did what we had set out to do. We each held the biggest rock we could carry. Manda, long brown hair rippling like a flag, yelled "DAM!" and as her voice echoed back at us, we dropped our rocks over the edge. Careening, cracking, and crashing off canyon walls, the boulders plummeted all three hundred and eighty-nine feet and then ricocheted off solid ice before coming to rest. The cacophony broke the silence fiercely; it was our favorite way to blow off steam. I exhaled.

As we slogged back to the learning center, I prayed the road would be cleared soon so I could get out of there. I longed for the diversions of the city – theater, art, lectures, movies, bookstores, dancing, hell even a mall was starting to sound fun.

When the weather cleared enough and road reports sounded promising, I would drive for two hours to the sleepy town of Mt. Vernon, to the health food coop or a coffee shop, just to see different faces from the handful I saw day-in and day-out. Longer trips to Bellingham or Seattle felt like pilgrimages to Disneyland.

The mountains were too quiet, too tame, and winter was stretching on forever. Out of boredom and the raw chill of a house with high ceilings and too many windows, I was often bundled in bed by eight.

One night, wide awake and watching the moon from the slit between down comforter to my nose and wool hat to my eyebrows, a lone coyote began to howl. I listened as he yelped and wailed alone in the night. No answer. Was he injured? Lost? What could be so terrible to elicit so mournful a cry? I wasn't sure, but I knew how he felt.

Spring brought some relief. When the snow receded enough for me to head out on the trails again my spirits lifted. But the bears, everywhere black bears! I used to love the solitude of hiking alone, but it seemed that every time I went out I would meet a bear, and the continual, fight-or-flight adrenaline was exhausting.

One afternoon, on a wander along Thunder Creek, I sat down for a rest on a log and started peeling an orange when a bear came crashing through the thicket right at me. My second encounter that day, I jumped up on the log, fists clenched, and shouted, "Leave me alone!" Which sent the bear running in the other direction, thankfully, but my hike was ruined. After that, every sound had me on edge, jittery. Fucking bears.

One rainy spring morning I led a group of sixth graders out onto the peninsula trail, telling them that if they stayed quiet we might spy one of the new fawns that had been seen there recently. Alert and eager, we swished around a corner in our raingear and then stopped short.

There on the trail in front of us lay a tiny spotted body with four knobby-kneed legs, petite hooves, and a bloody stump where a head used to be. Not quite the fawn sighting I'd had in mind. I hurried my charges off the peninsula, knowing the bear would be nearby and back for more, then sat them down to discuss the harsh realities of the food chain. A boy blinked back tears and looked away.

Early that summer as I attempted to wrangle a family group into lifejackets to head out for a canoe, a mother said to me, "You live in paradise." I recognized her wide-eyed awe as she looked up at the sun on the white peaks and the wind on the green water.

I squinted to see what she saw, but only noticed that the wind had picked up, proliferating swollen whitecaps. We would have to stick close to shore or perhaps not go out at all. I nodded absentmindedly and looked down at a raven picking at a fish carcass rotting in the shallows.

That June as I sat on my porch, swatting mosquitoes, I got a phone call from Ed, an old high school boyfriend. I was surprised he'd been able to track me down; though we were both from Connecticut, we had each leap-frogged all over the country since. After living as a ski bum in Colorado, he had become a kiteboarding bum in North Carolina. He called to tell me he was moving to Mexico.

When I told him I had planned to settle down but was having second thoughts, he told me the first thing that had made sense in a long time. He said, "Of course you are. You're like me— we're wanderers. We can't stop moving or we'll die."

I stared out the window at a tiger swallowtail lifting off a blade of grass and worried that he was right. Maybe I was a river that needed to keep flowing. Maybe someday I would reach the ocean that held the perfect blend of community and wilderness to sustain me, but I hadn't yet.

The North Cascades couldn't contain me. Warmed by the sun, I lifted off and away before summer's end.

The following summer I returned for a visit. I joined a group of families on a sunset walk to the dam and hung back to hear a new naturalist gush dam facts. As I stared out at the alpenglow above turquoise waters, I felt none of the divergent charge of my residency in the North Cascades. Just a tranquil calm.

Paradise or prison? It was both. It was the freshness and rose-colored glasses of a new love, the excitement of living a fantasy. And it was the harsh reality of a rugged hermit lifestyle and the trapped-animal feeling that comes with the word *forever*. Like the names of the peaks surrounding me, it was all of these things: Magic, Fury, Terror, Pinnacle, Damnation.

But those are just words on a postcard. The North Cascades are none of these things. Whatever we may see in the glassy green of Diablo Lake are simply reflections of our own minds. Whatever we may hear on the breeze or in the wail of a coyote are just the echoes of our own hearts.

Wilderness is *the Void* that we fill with paradise or prison, heaven or hell. A valley we can flow through or struggle against. Maybe one day I would learn how to live in the in-between place called home.

I flicked a pebble off the concrete railing of Diablo Dam, then turned to go before hearing it land.

Fast Freight

Suddenly I was wide-eyed and giddy, sniffing sweet sagebrush air, chuckling with a canyon wren's cartoon-like spiraling call from the rimrock cliffs above and sighing with the cerulean river rushing below. I was changed already, and I hadn't even left the parking lot.

Earlier that morning? I was shifty-eyed and growling, pacing and panting, irked by everyone and everything. The city was definitely too frenetic but my own four walls were closing in on me and even the forest felt claustrophobic. I was restless. Edgy. Agitated. Crazed. I stubbed my toe on a bookshelf and howled, kicked the wall for revenge. I spilled my coffee and slammed the mug down in the sink, chipping the glaze, then kicked the cabinet as punishment. I'm not sure for whom.

What was wrong? Nothing. Everything. Sometimes I don't bother asking why. Any justification seems arbitrary. My life was fine. Everything was fine. Just channeling my inner feral animal.

Again.

I was breathing easier now, no drug but a change of scenery, the landscape, and a day to myself. I stood in north central Oregon at the confluence of the Deschutes River and the Columbia, blue ribbons through golden hills stretching on into eternity. A cool morning breeze tickled a strand of hair against my neck and I scratched.

Was this enough? Could I sit by the river, read a book, scribble in my journal and go home?

Nope. This animal needed to move. Needed to keep moving. To get farther away from something, or maybe it was closer to something. Maybe both.

I hopped on my mountain bike and pedaled onto the Deschutes River Rail Trail. In front of me a dusty gravel bed cut through yellowed grasses and a few tardy sunflowers, on into the infinity of the horizon. Eleven miles to one suggested turn-around point, fifteen miles to the next, but the railroad grade continued ten miles beyond that, maybe twenty. Right then all I wanted to do was go, keep going.

It was a typical August day out there, sun already hot on bare arms at 9 a.m. with an expected high of one hundred and eight that afternoon. A few scraggly sagebrush and desiccated forbs carpeted the suntanned hills, not a tree in sight, and right then, that was exactly right. Right there, in all that expansiveness, was where I fit.

I pumped my legs to pick up speed over chunky gravel and my hair whipped against my neck. The trail climbed higher, away from the river, so all color and action receded. White motor boats, neon river rafters, bright blue water and tents in primary colors dotting the riverbank, all grew smaller. I rode on, deeper into the dusty heat, a sallow faded photograph of the Wild West. I was the action there, the big movement, the animation of a still life. I felt completely alone and therefore, totally free.

The long slow wail of a train whistle across the river reminded me of an old Kingston Trio song my dad used to sing to my sister, Becca, and me when we visited him in one of the various tucked away places he lived after he left. He sang a lot of folk songs back then, the hippie-turned-hermit, but this one was my favorite. *Sing the train song, Dad!* On his acoustic guitar, or occasionally his banjo, auburn hair and red beard ponytailed against the humid East Coast summer nights, he'd croon that melancholy dirge about riding the rails. About leaving the ones you love and never coming back. About the lonesome sound of the train whistle and the restless clickety clack of the wheels on the track.

Clickety clack? Sheesh, Dad. Never mind the parental strife, divorces, remarriages, relocations, and various other stressors of my youth. Never mind my own interpersonal challenges and sensitivities, my preference for flight over fight, or my continual fear that I'm settling, that I'm missing out on the bigger better thing somewhere else. I'm blaming my restlessness on *that* song.

No hoboing on this side of the river anymore; a mountain bike would have to do. The lore of the river valley tells that two competing railroad companies each started building infrastructure on opposite sides of the river, vying to be the first to connect the mighty Columbia River trade route to central Oregon. Each tried to sabotage the other, even, rumor has it, dynamiting the others' equipment. The west side Oregon Trunk Railroad won out, so I got to ride the nicely graded (so far) eastern gravel road that eventually peters off into nothingness where the Deschutes Railroad company finally gave up. I was literally on a road to nowhere. And there wasn't anywhere I'd rather be.

A few miles in, an old railroad car posed next to the trail, doors open and empty, sun shining through from the other side casting the only shadow for miles around. I hopped off my bike and stood in the coolness of its shade for a moment, looked through the frame to the river far below. I couldn't hear the river from there, couldn't hear anything. It was desert quiet, everything still, and the railroad car, bleached by sun and swept clean by wind, completed the movie-set feel of the landscape. When a tumbleweed blundered across the road ahead I was not surprised. I took the hint and pedaled on.

As I traveled on down the road, the road got rougher, less gravel and more chunky rock. As I traveled into midday the earth heated up, a warm wind wafted up the valley and evaporated my sweat before it materialized. Prairie grasses I couldn't imagine were ever green started to shimmy and shake along the road as cicadas tuned their voices with the grasshoppers. A kestrel appeared over the ridge and fluttered in place, "kiting," waiting for the right moment to dive. Rather than rest in the heat, that place turns on, wakes up. I sucked water from my CamelBak, tugged my baseball cap lower on my forehead and bumped on over rock. Soon I approached another railroad car, but that time, I kept moving. Clickety clack.

Around a bend, a house appeared. Just below the trail that was supposed to be a railroad, more than ten miles south of the highway on that roadless road, stood, barely, an abandoned house. Only the shell was intact; like the rail cars it was empty, clean, and open from one side to the other. A sagebrush-grey wooden roof with cracks between boards sagged against shrunken mud-colored plank walls at awkward angles, all somehow defying gravity and time and weather to remain generally vertical against yellow and brown hills beyond. No windows, no doors, only holes to the other side.

I began to hear a creaking, humming, moaning sound, and realized the house itself was singing. Wind whistled through wood to the train across the river and the train that no longer comes near, if it ever did. To the people who – like the song, like my dad – left and never came back. I stood right where I could stare through the house to the desert beyond. I stood in the sun and the heat and listened to the music.

The sun had crested the sky and I knew I should turn around soon, probably should have already turned around, considering the heat and my westside, pale-skinned, better-suited-to-mist-and-rain disposition and, more immediately, my nearly diminished water supply, but I couldn't. I physically couldn't turn back, not yet. I had to go forward, on past the wailing house and around the next bend. Even though I knew there would always be another next bend. Finding out what was there was more important than comfort or even safety. Maybe I'd find another haunted house, or maybe just more dust and rock and tumbleweeds. It didn't really matter. The point is, I'd know. I'd witness. So, onward.

I was drunk on sagebrush. A layer of dust had settled onto my skin on top of the third layer of sunscreen. Vanilla-scented ponderosa pines lined the trail, adding a little shade here and there, but also sharp-pointed cones everywhere, crunching under my tires. The rocks had grown bigger too, almost small boulders, barely suitable even for my mountain bike. The seedpods of some dried shrub rattled in the wind like rattlesnakes, or maybe those *were* rattlesnakes, and I flicked my eyes on the trail to make sure I didn't blunder over one coiled in the sun.

It must have been really hot then because the cicadas were fully revved up, emitting their highest pitched whine. A glossy black and white magpie swooped down in front of me and laughed when I jumped. I laughed back and stopped to watch it for a minute or maybe ten, and when I started to peddle again my shoelace caught on the pedal and I lost my balance, catching myself too late. I fell, tangled in my bike, onto sharp rocks. I was bleeding. Both legs, one hand, and an elbow.

I was still laughing.

Back on the road. Past a useless water tower, around the next bend. Into and out of more trees, around the next bend. Around a bend where a rockslide had almost completely obliterated the trail. Around and onward and forward and around again until I noticed a strange hissing sound right in front of me. Right under me, in fact.

Had I run over a rattlesnake?

No. That was my front tire, losing air. Quickly. Huh.

Okay, I guess *now* it was time to turn around. Fine. I faced back the way I came. Onward!

I must have been about twelve miles out and though the road was mostly level, twelve miles wasn't exactly a short walk in searing heat with almost no water. I decided to attempt to ride my hissing bike as far back as it would take me.

I made it back to the singing house before I discovered my back tire was flat too. Time to walk. I climbed off, lines of dry blood collecting dust down both stinging shins, and started walking. Still smiling.

If I was with people? I would have turned around long before. If I was with people I would not have been drizzled in dried blood, would have an intact bicycle, and would have been back at my car by then, fully hydrated and heading to a brewpub in Hood River to drink Hefeweizen with lemon from a frosty glass. I would have enjoyed pleasant conversation, making sure to speak up enough to remain interesting company. I would have enjoyed the camaraderie of a shared adventure, and probably noticed and learned some things I wouldn't have on my own. But I would have missed... this.

What exactly was this? Nothing. Everything.

Maybe I was delirious from the heat, from dehydration, from the ceaseless wind that was drying my lips like the parched landscape around me, cracked and dusty. From the miles to go to reach my car, and water, and, if I needed it, help. I knew I should have been worried. I dug out my cell phone and checked for service. No bars. I smiled.

My legs still worked. Plenty of daylight and, if need be, moonlight. The path was clear, stretching on ahead and around that next bend. And the next.

Why was it that out there, on the road/in the wilds/riding that trail/that train, I felt like I could handle whatever came my way, when just that morning I had a temper tantrum over a stubbed toe? I looked around for answers but there were only cicadas whining, dry grasses shimmying. The feral animal panted, wagged, urged me on.

That sun was getting a bit much. My permanent squint couldn't have been helping my emerging dehydration headache. Wait... where was my hat? I didn't remember having it since... since I fell, which was now a couple miles behind me. Couldn't go back for it. Always forward, only forward, which just happened to be a different direction, now.

I walked. Dragged my bike alongside me, lumpy rubber and rims bumping over rock. I walked on that dusty gravel bed that cut through yellowed grasses and a few tardy sunflowers. I walked through the heat and the grasshoppers that jumped out of my way and tumbleweeds that tickled my legs, hurrying the other direction. I walked on into the infinity of the horizon.

When I made it back to one of the railroad cars I dropped my bike and crawled up onto the smooth wood floor, lay back in the shade and let my legs hang off the side. I tilted my head to see behind me, out the other side of the car and down the hillside toward the blue of the river, probably only a mile below. I imagined the luscious cool of that water and considered abandoning my useless bike and hiking down the cliff to get there, maybe hitch a ride back from a motorboater... but knew I never would. I had to stay on the road. Stay on the rails. I'm no tumbleweed. Clickety clack, clickety clack.

Back on the road I was limping, arms sore from the weight of the bike and sweaty feet blistered in my shoes. I shook the last few hot drips of water into my mouth and kept moving. A far-off canyon wren sounded maniacal and the heat swirled liquid waves on the road ahead. I passed up the next rail car and instead slumped in the partial shade of a large sagebrush for a rest. I began to hear voices.

Neat—I was hallucinating.

Then I saw two forms moving toward me on the trail. I was flabbergasted, had forgotten this was a public trail and that other people might possibly be out enjoying a sweltering day in the desert far from the river. But sure enough, there they were, two normal-looking people, chatting and laughing and getting closer.

I scrambled to my feet, grabbed my bike and got moving again, slitting my eyes against the two approaching figures. I imagined how I must look and attempted to smooth my hair, brush off some of the dried blood, then gave up. I wasn't one of them, that day. That day I was a lone wolf, bloody and snarling. As we passed I turned up the corners of my mouth and waved but avoided eye contact and moved quickly past to avoid conversation.

At dusk I reached the campground where my car awaited. I was dusty, bloody, bruised, road-rashed, sunburned, lips cracked, dehydrated, and positively elated. I found a drinking-water pump and let it flow, let it wash over me and cool me and I drank until I thought I might puke and then drank some more.

I looked back at the road behind me. For a minute or ten I stood still and looked. Like the railroad cars, the abandoned house, that landscape, I was open, weathered, swept clean, and empty. I stood in north central Oregon at the confluence of the Deschutes River and the Columbia, blue ribbons through golden hills stretching on into eternity. A hot evening breeze tickled a strand of hair against my neck and I scratched.

Then I got moving. Lashed my bike to the car and got on the road to home. Back to the pack. Back to the long slow exhausting ride through our days together, where I've no choice but to move forward, always forward, on the road to nowhere. My father's voice in my head, clear and faint like a far-off train.

Prey

I slammed on the brakes and sat motionless in my idling Volkswagen. The animal must have been at least nine feet long from nose to tail, since it spanned almost the width of the mountain road. I held my breath, gripped the wheel, and gave thanks for the steel and glass barriers between me and that enormous feline.

Steady, unhurried, confident, it lifted one meaty paw after the other, long thick tail trailing behind. It was crossing the road less than fifteen feet in front of my car, yet it didn't acknowledge me.

In the waning sun spilling over the Rocky Mountain foothills, tawny fur shone like gold. Glinting amber eyes and black-tipped ears adorned a head that seemed too small for such a massive body. The whole effect was less like a lion, tiger, or any of the other big cats I'd seen in zoos, and more like a supersized housecat. The most elegant, magnificent, and righteously haughty cat I could imagine. The cattest of cats. Cougar.

As it stepped off the side of the road toward the aspen grove beyond, it turned and gave the briefest of glances in my general direction – though not at me – and leapt into my past. My fingers relaxed on the steering wheel but my heart continued to race. Foot steady on the brake, I pressed my forehead to the window and strained to see what was no longer there.

What was it I was feeling? I'd seen weasels, coyotes, foxes, even bobcats and black bears, but cougar felt... different.

~

Cougar. Mountain lion. Puma. Panther. Catamount. Deer tiger. Mountain screamer? *Puma concolor*, the Guinness world record holder for the animal with the most names, is North America's second largest feline. The largest – the jaguar – tends to stick to the lands from Mexico south. The more wide-ranging cougar can be found from northern British Columbia to the tip of South America; in the States it is most populous in the mountainous West where there are estimated to be more than 30,000.

Like all cats, cougar belongs to the Felidae family. Yet unlike the other big cats, the true lions and tigers, cougars do not belong to the subfamily Pantherinae. They are instead the largest members of Felinae. Which means that even the heftiest, two-hundred-pound males cannot roar. Instead, like your housecat, they growl, hiss, yowl, and purr.

Spotted cougar kittens stick with their mothers for a year, but adult life is mainly solitary. Males and females maintain separate, only slightly overlapping territories where they might meet for just one to six days a year to mate, and briefly at other times to warily, tentatively, share larger kills.

Each cougar prefers large areas of undisturbed wilderness, but in the western United States, where humans are spreading like kudzu, our ranges increasingly overlap. Though still relatively rare, human/cougar encounters are becoming more common.

~

In the foothills of Washington's central Cascade Range, a two-story garage-turned-apartment on a large estate backs up to a national forest. In one direction houses, roads, and people sprawl for thirty miles to Seattle. In the other direction trees, rivers, and ridges span for thirty miles to the crest of the Cascades. When I lived there, my bedroom window faced the wilds.

The landlords had a motion sensor light at the peak of the barn outside, trained on their horse corral below. At first I found the light annoying, as it was so near to my window that the click of it switching on and the sudden brightness were enough to wake me out of my typically light sleep. Until I realized it meant something was down there, something I would get to see if I was quick enough.

So. Each time I heard the click I would spring up, put on my glasses, and peer down into the spotlight. I got to spy on raccoons, opossums, blacktail deer, a coyote, the neighbor's housecat, and once a freakish stuffed clown my friends left as an April Fools' joke (as well as my retreating friends, who underestimated my speed of alertness).

Click. Light. Glasses. Window.

At 2 a.m. one spring night, under the pendulous green blooms of a bigleaf maple, there it was. As long as a length of the split-rail fence and almost as tall. Tense in the sudden brightness, one tan paw frozen in mid-air in front, tail horizontal behind, as if floating on water.

Time paused, snapping a picture. I stared unseen from my window, waiting. It twitched one ear, listening.

"Cougar!" I whispered. The sensor light clicked off.

If a cougar walks through a forest and no one is around to see it, does it exist? If I see a cougar but the cougar doesn't see me, do I exist?

Wide-eyed in the darkness, I couldn't fall back to sleep.

~

Among the high peaks of North Cascades National Park, thirty miles east of civilization, nestles a tiny village of environmental educators. It is one of the increasingly few places in the country more wild than human-inhabited. The year I lived there, deer wandered among us and a resident bobcat and multiple black bears made regular appearances. Still, we only knew of local cougars through their tracks in the snow and the occasional pile of scat. Their scat told us that in those mountains they stuck mainly to their preferred diet of deer. One prominent scat pile – in the middle of a well-used human trail – featured an intact deer hoof. For visiting fifth graders, the food chain lesson didn't get more experiential than that.

Though deer make up the bulk of cougars' diet, they will catch and eat most any animal they can. They are pure carnivores, and meat is meat. They will take rabbits, porcupines, grouse, rats, and yes, sometimes, house cats, dogs, and chickens. Hunters are opportunists. Choosing an easy kill is more than convenience; it can mean life or death. Should we blame them?

On a day off one summer morning I prepared to go for a hike. The sky wore a cobalt blue only the mountains and arid east side of the Cascades can offer, with the kind of dry heat that drinks your sweat faster than you can produce it.

As I walked to the desk by my second-story window to grab my sunglasses, movement outside caught my eye. Looking down I immediately recognized that round head, beefy body, and impossibly long tail of the mountain lion. This time in full daylight.

It had just come up the bank from the river and, muscled shoulder-blades and hipbones moving rhythmically, was strutting toward a rocky ridge.

I sucked in my breath but forgot that my window was open, so it heard me. Its head whipped toward the house. Wanting to hold on to the moment longer, forever, I turned to grab my camera. When I turned back to the window, the cougar was gone.

I ran outside with the idea of following, then feeling vulnerable, ran back inside, grabbed a broom and went back out again. I searched the ridge above the cabin where it was headed, then the cottonwood grove by the river from whence it had come and found nothing. No sign, not one track. The cougar had vanished.

How often do they move among us, like ghosts, unseen?

~

Not all sightings are benign. Humans do get attacked, particularly when wandering alone at dawn or dusk, or while running or biking, which can trigger a chase response. What surprises me is how seldom this occurs, typically less than five times a year in all of North America. Yet we are perfectly deer-sized, and far less agile or aware of our surroundings. And increasingly more populous than deer. Endless expansive colonies teeming with meaty morsels. Easy meals.

It would be so simple. A cougar is a master of patience, stealth, and surprise. Its preferred hunting method is to wait in a tree or on a rocky ledge until the moment prey is below and then leap onto its shoulders and bite the back of its neck. Sharp canines are perfectly spaced to span cervical vertebrae and slice into the spinal cords of deer, paralyzing them instantly. Compare your neck to a deer's neck. Exactly.

Though anywhere between seventy to two-hundred

pounds, even a smaller cougar can take an adult elk or small moose this way. But cougars can also sprint thirty-five miles per hour, and with muscled back legs like giant jackrabbits can leap thirty feet in one bound. Super-predators.

~

At 8,000 feet in the Colorado Rocky Mountain foothills a studio apartment sits back from the main house on the road. This log shed-like lean-to was built into the side of a rocky ridge at the edge of a grove of ponderosa pines. I lived there too, in the heart of cougar country. I had already seen two crossing the road, and knew from my job at Colorado Parks and Wildlife that there were frequent sightings in the area.

In the midnight darkness one October I parked my car by the road and began the walk to my cabin. With the penlight on my keychain I projected a tiny beam into the darkness and swept it to either side of the stone walkway. Night was quiet there, always so quiet compared to the cricket and frog serenades of the wetter environments I'd inhabited. I'd heard occasional coyotes or if I was lucky, a great-horned owl, but usually, silence.

I passed the landlords' dark house and continued toward my home. When I was just a few steps from the door my little penlight caught something shining above me. Eye-shine. Above me. I froze, then pointed my light up at a cougar, fifteen feet away on my roof.

She looked right at me.

It would have been so easy, barely a step down off the low roof onto me, teeth sunk into my neck. But I didn't think about that, not then. I looked back at her. She was the most beautiful animal I'd ever seen. Lying with both paws in front of her, alert and regal as a sphinx. Calm. Fearless. Her eyes burned into me.

As far as humans have come in world domination and how

strongly we believe we are apex predators, we are nothing of the sort. We may be hunters but we are no predators, not like that. Mostly we are smart, sneaky scavengers. We are wily coyotes and crows and rats and dogs but we are no mountain lions. Locked in her gaze I was put in my place like never before. Suddenly, I understood what it was I had been struggling to grasp.

I knew without a doubt that I am prey.

There was no fight or flight. There was only submission.

Then a tiny voice deep inside reminded me, *move.* I yanked my eyes away and took the final few steps underneath her and into my front door.

Did she coil up on her haunches to pounce, or did she remain there, watching me go? I will never know.

Only when the door shut behind me did I recognize the thing called fear. Or maybe it is called exhilaration. Right then that thing was in my body, from tingling scalp to thumping heart to clenched fists and I don't care what you call it.

I didn't turn on the light but flew to the back window. After a few seconds I heard heavy steps above me and then the thud of her landing in the darkness. I saw only the dark tip of her tail swish in the shadows as she trotted into the pines.

~

The frequency of my cougar encounters some would say is dumb luck. Just living in high-density cougar areas and getting out in the wilds away from the crowds doesn't explain it. Few in the same situations will ever see one. Some would say it is meaningful, symbolic. Something about coming into my power, asserting my strength. Neither feels quite right to me.

I like to joke with my friends that cougars are stalking me. Me, personally. Rather self-important of me, I know. But I do feel like a chosen one. I would like to be a chosen one. I feel no shame in being prey, not for so worthy a predator.

One snowy afternoon two months later I sprawled on my bed with a book. It was one of those Rocky Mountain midwinter days where the air is so cold and still that the snow doesn't really fall but sort of floats around.

Then...familiar heavy footsteps on my roof.

I jumped up and peered out the back window. *Thump*, down it came. A slightly smaller body with faint spots, but even bigger feet and a longer tail. A juvenile. The kin of my first visitor? Her offspring?

Did she lead him to me?

He took a few steps toward the pines, each foot replacing the one before as a cat does to avoid stepping deeper into snow. Then he stopped, sniffing the air.

Forehead against the window, I burned my gaze into the back of his neck.

Cougar. Listen. I will not go without a fight. But. If you do sink your teeth into me and tear me apart, consume all that I am, then will I see through your eyes?

The Road Well-Traveled

I-84 West
The Subaru didn't feel like mine, even as I drove it away from the Connecticut house toward my home in the West. The interior smelled of my mother's perfume, which would take a couple years to fully fade from the grey vinyl. My mother knew my VW was on its last legs. She could afford a new car. She knew I could not. I was indebted to her for the gift. Beholden. Bound. I love her and hated that.

I'd flown in for a quick visit and to help move my grandmother from her retirement community to a nursing home. The back of my mother's old station wagon now held other hand-me-downs, a cedar blanket chest my mother no longer wanted and faux crystal dishes my grandmother no longer needed. I left the rest behind. The verdant hues of suburban lawns, white-picket fenced. White-painted houses with black trim, American flags by the front door. Home-cooked meals, attentiveness, selflessness. Sacrifice, placation, duty. Predictability.

I pushed the pedal to the floor; I was speeding. Out of Connecticut – that happens fast – into and out of New York, and into Pennsylvania. I could still smell my mother.

I-80 West

I can't remember how many times I've crossed the country. Cars, moving trucks, southern route, northern route, solo or with friends. Campgrounds, motels, rustic cabins. The thrilling freedom of the open road. The feeling of possibility, life unscripted.

Now, there was no time. Too few vacation days between family back East and work out West. I drove to get there. It still felt like freedom, just faster. I held the wheel, pressed the gas. I was in control.

To save money, I slept in the car. I spooned the blanket chest for a few hours in an Indiana truck stop, until the semi-trucks roared into my dreams and the streetlights blazed through my eyelids and I gave up, bought a cup of battery acid coffee at the all-night convenience store and drove on.

I-90 West

Steely thunderclouds rolled and purple lightning flashed over rippling grain – or was it corn? – and though I was white-knuckling the steering wheel I'd rather be there, wherever I was, somewhere in the middle, than mired in the burdens behind and ahead. There, I had nothing to do but drive.

Highway, gas station, highway. Sleep deprivation and caffeine jitters. I still had fruit, raw veggies, crackers and cheese, but fast food went down easier then. The open road demanded greasy heat.

"Life in the fast lane," I sang until my voice was hoarse, sang along to the classic rock I'd normally turn up my nose at—

the Eagles, Steve Miller Band—just to stay awake, because out there it was either that or country and no Yankee in her right mind will willingly listen to country. So it was "Fly like an eagle" and I was in the zone. I could drive forever. Maybe I would.

I-94 West

Must sleep. Car parked but still felt like I was moving, like too long in the waves. So cold. Still winter there. Closed my eyes, opened them two hours later. Trucks roared, lights shone. Teeth chattered. Ignition, heat, drive on.

Exit 32, western North Dakota rest stop. Looked like bathroom only, would have to wait for coffee. It was getting light anyway; that was a comfort.

But. What?

The hell.

Is that?

A mocha-brown behemoth loomed near the bathroom door. A statue? But it was moving, grazing. Not a cow. It was a... buffalo? Bison? So close, too close. I really had to pee. I looked around. Nobody. I listened. Munching grass. Wind across the plains.

I slunk past the animal into the steel and stone bathroom. Flushed, washed, warmed my hands under the blower. Opened the door, eyed the bison, skulked back to the warm car. *Want coffee.*

I-90 West

Wait a minute. Was there really a buffalo by that bathroom? *Think. Remember.* Expansive sky, light and shadows of dawn. Painted desert hills in the distance but not parched like Arizona or eastern Oregon; these valleys carpeted green. Thick, luxurious grasses from snowmelt and early spring rains, lush green stretching on into eternity. And, there, the hulking brown beast with ivory horns. Impossibly large and thick, the animal version of a giant sequoia. Head the size of my torso, dewy nose pointed down, snuffling munching sounds, a slight musky odor. By the bathroom.

Somehow time slowed to a stop, there, even as I moved on.

US-395 South

In Washington, almost home, I thought of the bison. Of those tranquil green plains and the wild brown animal, symbol of the untamed West.

I would learn later that I had stopped at the Painted Canyon Visitor Center of Theodore Roosevelt National Park. Would learn that my bison was a numbered member of a reintroduced and well-managed flock of cattle. Buffalo who may roam, but only within the confines of their fences.

I-84 West

Home again, to a soft bed, real food, routines, and responsibilities. Beholden to work and time.

Before long I would think again about escaping, leaving it all behind. Bison and I, we could go, look for freedom beyond the fences. Maybe it doesn't matter that what we're looking for doesn't exist anymore. Or that wherever we go, our pasts will trail us like perfume.

On the road, anything can happen. Sometimes, where you least expect it, it does.

Destiny Manifested

"Find your place on the planet. Dig in, and take responsibility from there."

—Gary Snyder

I'm a nomadic mutt from a long line of nomadic mutts. Nobody pointed a gnarled finger at the earth and told me: *This place, this landscape is where your people are from and where you belong.* When your people are from all over Europe, and more recently, all over the U.S. and Canada, when your family moves more often than most people wear out their favorite shoes, you wonder whether you have your own place on the planet.

After growing up in various towns in New England and getting a psychology degree in Virginia, my own wanderlust led me to Utah, Nevada, Florida, back north to New Hampshire for graduate school, to Oregon, Colorado, Washington, back to Oregon, back to Washington. Then Oregon.

~

Dr. Simeon Edward Josephi was born in New York City in 1849 of a Russian father and Spanish mother. "When I was 17 years old I had a bad attack of wanderlust. I wanted to see the world, so I went out to San Francisco to visit my brother David," he said in a 1926 interview in *The Oregon Journal*.

San Francisco didn't hold him for long; a year later he boarded a steamship north up the coast and east up the Columbia River to Portland. Arriving in a rainstorm, Josephi rode via horse and buggy then ferry to the east side of the Willamette River, East Portland. "In those days the ferry ran only during daylight. If you wanted to cross the Willamette after dusk you stood on the bank and called across to the ferryman, who came over in a rowboat to get you."

Josephi studied psychological medicine and became a doctor at the Hawthorne "hospital for the insane." He eventually took over as superintendent of the hospital, ran a private practice in downtown Portland, and became a professor of nervous and mental diseases at Willamette University and University of Oregon. He continued to live in East Portland where he married and fathered five children. "When I came to Portland on February 4th, 1867, I had no intention of staying here more than six months." He died in Oregon in 1935.

~

I first moved to Oregon on a whim. After completing a master of science degree in environmental biology I found I had a deep understanding of the ecology of New England and still no desire to make a home there. I didn't feel like a master of anything and knew I had more to learn somewhere else. A close friend's sister was moving to Portland for graduate school and neither my friend, Amanda, nor I had anything keeping us on the East Coast, so one humid day in August 2000 we loaded a taxi-yellow Penske and hit the interstate. I figured I would stay for a year or two, until the winds blew me elsewhere.

I'd never been to Oregon but I knew enough to pronounce it correctly, not *Ori-gone* like my Yankee friends would say. My father's father had retired to the Oregon Coast and my uncle had moved there to care for him as he aged, but I barely knew either of them. My father spent a few summers there as a kid visiting his grandparents and, based on his stories and pictures, I was pretty sure the whole Pacific Northwest was a mythic fairyland, a wilder, grander, wilier version of the Northeast, a place where forests sprawled farther than cities and emerald mists were so enchanting I wouldn't even care that it rained all the time.

After a two-week cross-country adventure with extended stays in the western wonders of Badlands and Yellowstone National Parks, I worried Oregon would be a disappointment. But on that final leg of the journey on Interstate 84 as our trusty Penske entered the Columbia River Gorge, as the sun beamed spotlights on glowing snow-capped Mt. Hood, Douglas fir-crowned cliffs, Western redcedar valleys, and resplendent waterfalls cascading toward the mighty Columbia, I was smitten. "I can't believe we live here now!"

~

Harvey L. Clark was born in Vermont in 1807, but in 1840 traveled overland with his wife, Emeline, to Oregon. After moving around the Willamette Valley as a Methodist missionary, Clark made a land claim in an area southwest of Portland that would become Forest Grove. He and his wife started a school for Native Americans and later, a home for orphans. His strong belief in education led him to donate two hundred and twenty acres of his land claim to help found a college, first called Tualatin Academy and later, Pacific University. The Clarks had three children and died in Oregon.

~

How can a place 3,083 miles from where you are born feel like home before you've even finished unpacking? The city of Portland was progressive, hip, culturally interesting and suited me well, but the flora and fauna of the surrounding landscape stole my heart. I hiked volcanic peaks, swam in icy snowmelt rivers, frolicked in fern-frosted forests, and jumped waves in the Pacific. I went on bird walks, plant walks, mushroom walks and moss walks and still I couldn't get enough of Cascadia. I wanted to learn more, understand better. It wasn't the curiosity of a tourist, but the growing devotion of a citizen.

Some combination of smells, sounds, and sensations in Pacific Northwest ecosystems fed me in a way that nowhere else had. Maybe my ecology background inspired me to connect with the natural landscapes, or maybe in my late twenties I was just ready to drop anchor somewhere, anywhere. But in recent travels I'd visited other beautiful places near interesting cities – New Orleans, Santa Fe, Flagstaff, Salt Lake City, Missoula, San Francisco – why not any of these? Outside of jobs or relationships, when we have the freedom, why do we leave a place? Or, why do we stay?

My sister, Becca, in her wanderings, moved to Oregon shortly after I did. Then my father, so for a few short years all the living Durhams of my immediate family lived in Oregon. But then my grandfather died, Becca moved east to Montana followed by my father, and my uncle got busy starting his own family at the Oregon coast. My friend Amanda returned to Connecticut and her sister moved east to Washington, D.C. I remained.

To me, the Northwest wasn't about family. It was about a rugged individualism and connection with wild nature, like the Scottish naturalists John Muir and David Douglas. I was named for a Scottish wildflower, a hardy, shrubby thing of alpine cliffs and rain-soaked bogs.

~

Douglas Cameron Ingram was born in 1882 in Scotland and moved to Oregon at nineteen, in 1901. A U.S. Forest Service ranger and ecologist, he was also a devoted botanist, collecting plants for the USFS herbarium from all over Oregon and Washington, including two rare subspecies named for him: Ingram Columbia Lily (*Lilium columbianum Hanson var. ingramii*) and Ingram's Indian Pink (*Silene hookeri var. ingramii*). The latter is a rare alpine flower found only in Oregon.

In August 1929 he was sent to Okanagan, Washington to help lead a fire crew fighting the 23,000-acre Camas Creek wildfire. When the wind changed and the fire spread, he met his death in a wall of flames. A ridge in that area northeast of Lake Chelan now bears the name "Douglas Ingram Ridge." Before he died, he and his wife, Emogene, had one daughter, Alice. They lived in Oregon.

~

I moved away from Oregon after five years. A relationship had ended badly and I thought a change of scenery would do me good. I settled on Boulder, Colorado, deciding that this other progressive, hip, culturally interesting city on the edge of the Rocky Mountains could be my new home. But immediately, confusingly, I was homesick. I tried to be at home there, for two years I tried. Until I gave up and moved to Washington. And then back to Oregon. And back and forth again, like a pendulum slowing to rest.

Only after leaving did I understand what home really means, that certain comfort and contentedness that goes deeper than familiarity. In Colorado I felt away from the center, outside, gone. Not *there*. The Pacific Northwest held a strong sense of being and belonging, *here*.

I've been back for ten years, a long time for a nomad but not so long in the scope of a life. I can't be sure I will stay forever. But I am digging in.

For several years I worked in ecological restoration, acting as doctor, teacher, and steward of the natural landscapes I love. In my employment with Portland-based nonprofit Friends of Trees, I worked in natural areas around Portland as well as in outer suburbs from the Columbia Gorge to Forest Grove, leading volunteer tree planting projects.

One year I stood on the rain-soaked lawn of a public park in front of eighty or so eager volunteers while the mayor of the little town spoke of the park's history and the good work we were about to do. It was the usual pre-planting pomp and circumstance and I was only half listening, thinking of all I needed to do to facilitate the process of helping novice planters get eight hundred new trees planted in the riparian buffer of Fanno Creek in the next three hours. Waiting for my turn to speak, I watched robins tilt their heads to spy worms in the soil and listened to goldfinches singing from trees and shrubs planted by volunteers in previous years.

Then the mayor spoke a name that jolted me out of my head. Suddenly I was blushing and grinning as if I had just been handed an award. Albert Alonzo Durham. My great, great, great grandfather.

~

Albert Alonzo Durham was born in Oswego, New York, in 1814 and moved to Oregon in 1847. He claimed land and built a homestead in an area south of Portland that would be named Lake Oswego. There he built a sawmill, advertising his lumber in the first issue of the weekly *Oregonian*. In 1866 he sold the mill and moved to the west side of the Willamette where he built a new sawmill and a flour mill on Fanno Creek. Locals referred to the area as "Durham Mills." It was later incorporated into the tiny town of Durham.

A.A. Durham, as he was known, was father to George H. Durham.

George H. Durham married Satira Emeline Clark, daughter of Pacific University's founder, Harvey Clark, of Forest Grove, Oregon. Their son was George C. Durham.

George C. Durham married Mary Helen Josephi, daughter of Dr. Simeon Josephi of East Portland, Oregon. Their son was George S. Durham.

George S. Durham married Alice Ingram, daughter of Forest Service botanist Douglas Ingram. Their son was George I. Durham.

George I. Durham married my mother, and had me.

~

I knew all this, long ago. Back when Oregon was still the mystical fairyland *Out West*, the land of my father's people for several generations before my grandfather moved east in a reverse migration and I was born a Yankee. Even after first moving to Oregon, after visiting ancestral places and smiling every time I saw the road sign for Durham, even after leading a restoration project in a place my coworkers and I jokingly called "my park," my multiple familial connections to Oregon and Washington never seemed more than amusing anecdotes. We all have family from somewhere; who cares?

When the mayor of Durham spoke of the great man who founded his town and turned my insides all warm and mushy, I guess that was me starting to care.

I didn't say anything to the mayor right then, and since I was standing slightly behind him, he didn't notice my emotional flare-up. If he did, he wouldn't have understood anyway—he didn't know me. But after the planting started, I pulled him aside and said, "You know, I have an interesting story for you..." And then there was the mayor shaking *my* hand like *I* was the celebrity, saying I should stop by city hall sometime.

It would be several more months before I realized the karmic symmetry of my work in Durham City Park. How Albert Alonzo cut trees down and how I planted them, possibly in the same exact place. More time would pass before I visited the family plot in the Portland cemetery that sits on a hill just across the Willamette River from where I was living in East Portland, to peer at the graves of the three Georges before my father. What did begin in me that morning in Durham City Park was the new and strange feeling of an ancestral family home.

I can't know why my ancestors were drawn here or what made them stay. But they are part of the reason I am here. In Oregon and Washington, my ancestors are thick as old-growth trees. If I could condense all times to now, I'd be surrounded by family. The men whose stories I know, and all the men and women whose stories I don't.

Maybe it's biological – something in my genes, the nature of my body carrying bits of all of them – Clark, Josephi, Ingram, and Durham – maybe stronger in me than in my father and sister pulled elsewhere by different genetic expression, different familial blood. Maybe blood is thicker than the waters of our birthplaces. This place, this landscape, is where my people are from.

Does it follow, then, that this is where I belong?

As much as I'd like to believe that, I can't. I don't.

What right did my ancestors have to be here, a place that already belonged, by all definitions but their own, to others? Did my European ancestors believe in a God-ordained destiny to move west, to colonize these lands? Did they believe it was theirs for the taking, with no thought of the people they took from, those who had been here not for dozens or hundreds but thousands of years before them? As much as I'd like to believe, not *my* family, not *my* blood, the language in the family archives suggests otherwise. To "claim," to "discover," to "settle." Read: to take, to erase, to displace. Their blood is on my hands too.

What right do I have to be here?

None.

So. What do I do with that? How can I possibly belong here, now? Should I, instead, return to the Scotland, Ireland, or Western Europe of my ancestors? I can't pretend to belong there either, not anymore. Not that they'd take us back anyway, especially these days.

Perhaps, instead, I can accept that I may not ever belong here, not in the same way as the people whose names I've spoken far more often than that of the stolen Oregon mill town. Multnomah, Tualatin, Clackamas, Chinook. Skagit, Snoqualmie, Snohomish, Salish...

Still somehow, more than anywhere else, these names have come to embody my place on this planet. Not mine because I've taken land, renamed plants, founded schools or towns. Not mine by ownership or birthright or ancestral roots. Mine only in the small way that with time, curiosity, devotion, and immersion, something of these lands got into me. *I* feel bound to *them*. I belong *to* this landscape. And I intend to do right by it. To understand that with this sort of belonging comes responsibility. As naturalist, as steward, as a lover of the Pacific Northwest, I have a responsibility to my ancestors, yes, but also to the people who came before, and to the land itself. A duty, a destiny even, to speak *all* the names, to learn *all* the stories of my chosen home.

Part 3: Immersions

Love Letters

Dear New England,

You were my first. The first time I looked outside of myself and into the depths of another. And what depths you held! From your cranberry bogs and beaver ponds crawling with spotted salamanders, wood frogs, and spring peepers, to your weathered granite mountains scrubby with juniper and wild blueberries, and every pine, maple, oak, birch, and beech forest in between.

You had your crotchety side, of course, you old Yankee, with your poison ivy, mosquitoes, and blackflies. Your sticky summer humidity and thunderstorm tantrums and raw winter cold and ice storms. But that just made you more real, more approachable. I never had to be perfect around you.

You had your lighter side too, always knew how to reach out and disrupt my adolescent brooding. Spindly hemlocks growing right out of boulders. Porcupines waddling across trails. The mechanical fluting spiraling song of the veery. Fireflies and heat lightning. The root beer taste of yellow birch bark and wintergreen berries scattered like candies under the pines.

You're an old soul, despite your youthful exterior. One has to look closely to see your scars – healed cuts and burns, wagon wheel gouges through woodlands on long-abandoned trails. Crumbling stone walls, forgotten covered wells, foundation holes, and ancient arthritic apple trees in disappearing rows among the dense understory. What you don't know is that this is what makes you most beautiful to me. Yes, your fall colors are spectacular, all the blazing hues of fire fluttering on the breeze against the bluest sky above pumpkins and hayfields and milk cows and red barns and white farmhouses where cardinals and bluebirds whistle and flirt; you always did know how to paint a pretty picture. But I always preferred your subtler hues, your messy insides, from a disintegrating tire swing hanging from a frayed rope on that thick old wolf tree in the middle of the peeling birch grove where the secretive wood thrushes and warblers sing. Only there did I feel safe to open up and show you my own messy insides, my own truest self.

I sometimes wonder why you weren't enough. I had to leave, of course, had to head out on my own and start fresh, know others. We both knew I wasn't ready to settle down. But I thought I would come back to you. I assumed it for so long that it took me by surprise recently to realize I don't think I ever will. Though I continually look for you in others, I know I can never go back to who I was with you, what we were together. But you will always be the first, and all those who come after will forever have to measure up.

Dear Florida,
Let's be honest; neither of us was looking for something serious. It was a fling, that's all. Nothing wrong with that! What fun I had with you, running on the beach, frolicking in your tepid waves,

wandering half-naked in the moonlight in December. December! Christmas lights on palm trees.

Maybe I should have taken you more seriously. I did glimpse your introspective, brooding side, your resonant jungles where slinky snake-like anhingas swam among the mangrove roots and barred owls flew by day. Where black-crowned night herons posed motionless like reapers and alligators leered in the murky, mosquito-thick air.

But come on, those goofy pelicans? Scarlet ibis? Roseate spoonbills? Manatees! Technicolor parrots squawking at stoplights! Grinning dolphins choreographing water ballets! How gaudy, how flamboyant could you get? In fact, now that I think of it, I'm pretty sure you were gay. No biggie; I was too. That's probably why we got along so well. Anyway, I know I said I would call, or at least write, but you know how it goes.

Dear Desert Southwest,

I never meant to fall for you. But from the moment I laid eyes on you, inhaled your sagebrush cologne, ran my fingers over your smooth red curves, I was a goner. It was the sort of immediate, intense desire that quickly turns to heartbreak because I feared we would never be together. We were too different. I, too closed up, too stiff, too cold. You, completely open, so sensual, so exotic. Why would you ever want me?

I sought you out repeatedly over the years – wandered among prickly poppies in your shaded arroyos, climbed your canyon walls, rested still as a cactus atop cinder cones – yet you were always beyond my grasp. I felt your hot breath on my neck, strained my ears to hear you whisper your delicious, liquid poetry – *sonora, palo verde, ocotillo, saguaro* – but when I turned to look you were gone, and there was only rock and sand and sky, like an unfinished painting.

What a confusing mix of emotions you evoke in me. You

have the capacity to soothe, lull me into languid catatonia, while at the same time tossing me into existential crisis. I forget what I should be doing and even who I am around you, so I do nothing, am no one. You always leave me thirsty, sere and horny as your lizards. I ache to hold you close but your thorns repel me. I burn to lay in your arms though my head throbs, my skin flushes scarlet then peels away.

I like to think of you as the one who got away, but who am I kidding? I never had you in the first place.

Dear Arid Wild West,
Let me apologize right now. I never took you seriously, can't seem to see you as a three-dimensional whole. It's not that I didn't try. I gave myself to you wholeheartedly, left everything and everyone behind to start over with you, more than once. I inhaled the vanilla musk of your ponderosa pines, frolicked with your aspens by the riverbanks, and delighted in the song of your meadowlarks. I not only lazed around in your colorful summer garments – purple lupines, red Indian paintbrush, yellow lomatium, bluebells – I stuck around through your epic, snowbound, frigid winter whites.

You rebellious teenager mixed with Zen master, you macho cowboy mixed with wise ancestral elder, all this I saw, and still, somehow, you remain as a picture postcard to me. An idea, an ideal, a fantasy. Too many old movies, I guess. All I ever really wanted from you was your rough side. Rugged, wild, dry and scratchy like stubble. Your cracked skin. Your aloof, thin air, your need of space, so much space. Too much space. You unravel me, untether me, dry me out and shake me out of my bad habits. You help me gain perspective. And then I have to leave again.

You were the rebound, the one to escape to, a place to hide out from real life. I guess what I'm saying is, I used you. I've always used you. And if you'll let me, I will again.

Dear Pacific Northwest,

Darling Cascadia, you have my heart. Somehow you always have. Was I enraptured by my father's tales of shimmering fern-carpeted forests, the poster of your wild rocky coast on the wall of his Massachusetts home? Or long before that, generations of his family settled along your salmon-swirling rivers, my DNA rooted into your western redcedars? How could I ever get to know you on my own terms, beyond the fantasy?

Oh, but I did. I do!

We took it slowly at first – I needed that – courting, flirting, never speaking of commitment. And maybe because of that, because I was sure that it wouldn't last, I explored you with all my senses. Ogled all your spring greens and kept watching as you blushed and undressed in autumn. Inhaled your sweet cedar perfume that perfectly complements both your dry summer heat and cleansing winter rains. Fingered pungent amber cottonwood resins and tasted luminous raindrops poised on elastic lichens.

Maybe it's because I've taken the time to really know you, but you seem more deep, more complex than any who came before. Your intricacies rival even New England, though I recognize in you elements of all those who came before you. Rugged mountains softened with delicate wildflowers, basalt lava rock rivers trailing from volcanic peaks, pelicans diving along salty shores, and dense woodlands thick with warblers. And yet you offer so much that is uniquely you. Waterfall mists on my cheeks. Colossal trees I can't wrap my arms around in a genuine rainforest. Emerald moss-robed maples with leaves bigger than my face. Humble diminutive calypso orchids and ominous spiky devil's club. And the pinnacles of your wildness – bald eagles common as ravens, peregrine falcons roosting on cliffs. Salmon runs and bears. Mountain lions. Wolves!

Your moods fit my energies perfectly, ever inviting me in instead of making me want to escape as others have. Winter rains that tame my mania and encourage me to go inward, to sit still and read and write, think and sleep. Your summer sunshine, fresh and clear, encouraging me to hike and swim, romp and play. And all your pensive, restless, erratic moods in between, matching my own. Finding you in adulthood felt like discovering paradise and at the same time, like coming home.

Forgive me for taking so long to figure it out. In matters of the heart I'm a slow learner. It took me years and multiple separations before I even began to glimpse the truth. That maybe, just maybe, I wasn't destined to wander alone for all my days. That maybe I could stay with you and continue to be inspired, nourished, comforted, even stimulated. Finally, now, I can admit it. I've found my true love. For as long as we both shall live, 'til death do us part.

Blind

Welcome. Please put on your blindfold, meet in our classroom and help get a friction fire going. Keep your blindfold on until further notice.

The black Sharpie scrawl on a torn piece of notebook paper was taped to a stick speared into the ground in the middle of the trail, so we couldn't miss it. Ahead of me an eighteen-year-old and a sixty-five-year-old high-stepped along the wooded path, arms out and silent, onto school grounds. Behind me, more fellow students tumbled out of cars, sipped coffee from travel mugs and tucked water bottles into backpacks. These were the last images I would see for five hours and thirty minutes.

I didn't hesitate. I fished my bandana – one of the required school supplies – out of my daypack, knotted it at the back of my head and pulled my ears out from under it so my hearing would be intact. Backpack zipped and secured around my shoulders, I stepped forward onto the trail.

This was not the first time I'd been blind.

Why do we go to school? As children, for the most part, we were sent there. Whether we loved it, hated it, or accepted it without question, it's just something most of us did. We sat at our desks in rows inside square cinderblock rooms and got socialized in the business of the modern human world: reading, writing, science, and math. Human history, political science, sociology, and business management. And the less formalized but equally formative aspects of the curriculum: lunchroom and playground dynamics, team sports, clubs, school dances, birthday parties, and other flock activities.

If we are lucky we attend college and maybe graduate school. We learn how to belong as humans in society, adults with careers and families and social engagements with other humans. Lunchroom and office dynamics, dating, nightclubs, potlucks, dinner parties, parenting, and other flock activities. If we are adept at this business of being a human in society, the path can be a relatively straightforward one.

And then there are those of us who find ourselves at thirty-four years old, standing sightless in a rainforest in the foothills of the Washington Cascades Mountains, 3,000 miles from where we were born.

I raised one hand palm out a few inches in front of my face and positioned the other farther ahead in front of my stomach. I was relaxed as I began to take one confident step after another, drawing each foot up high and then gently down, feeling through my shoes the gravel of the parking lot and then the spongier woodchip surface of the trail.

Slight curve to the right, here, where the sword ferns brush my legs.

How many times had I walked blindfolded in the woods? Too many to count, from summer camp trust walks at age ten and adult teambuilding trainings at outdoor schools in multiple states, to this wilderness immersion program.

The cedar grove, sweet and pungent, is over there, but the trail here is lined with salmonberry brambles, so I best stick to the middle.

I'd walked this path dozens of times, perhaps hundreds, over the previous eight months.

Reach up to find the low-growing vine maple branch near the Pacific wren nest and duck under it, now.

I did not question the instructions nor worry what was ahead of me. I moved with the swiftness of experience.

Sharp right turn toward the sounds of community, and find my place among the other adults in the circle.

There are times in life when you know, even when you cannot see, that you are on the right path.

The open-air hut with the cool earthen floor was loud and chaotic – a frenzy of voices vying to be heard, nervous squeals and befuddled guffaws. The loudest, the extroverts, the natural leaders ruled. The confusing noise diminished me to meekness.

Blindfolded, I could handle. Alone in the woods, no problem. Human interaction? I didn't exactly have that figured out yet.

I attempted one offer of assistance from my perch on the encircling bench. "Um, hi? This is Heather... if anyone needs any help with anything, let me know..."

Hearing no reply, I resumed my place in the background, feeling more than usually invisible. Feeling as if I'd disappeared. I held on to my arms, resisting the urge to peek under my blindfold. My discomfort began to edge toward panic.

I was six years old again, climbing onto a school bus full of strange faces. I was twelve, in another new town, not cool enough to fit in. I was twenty, thirty. New. Scared. Outsider. Blind.

Then, a soft pat on my arm from the bench next to me. "Hi Heather."

I reached out, touched wiry greying curls and an Irish cable knit sweater I recognized. *Oh, my friend Georgia.* I felt the warmth of her shoulder against my own. Right, I knew these people. They knew me. I probably wasn't the only one having a hard time. Okay, it was going to be okay.

I leaned against a log post that supported the canvas walls, hugged my knees to my chest and listened. Voices, familiar, I named in my head. Carolyn. Lily. Jeff. Forest noises – birds, trees, and waters – I named them too. Chickadee. Bigleaf maple. Rain. The thunk of the axe through a log: someone chopping firewood in the yard outside. One of our instructors, Marcus, giving direction to keep folks safe while using their knives to carve kindling. Sticks snapped. Friction fire tools squeaked. I smelled cedar shavings, wet earth, someone's coffee, then smoke. The crack of ember giving way to flame and sparking cedar warmth. Finally, the din quieted and we all settled in to listen to our teachers tell tracking stories. Earth stories. I breathed slower, easier.

The afternoon held more active adventures, new challenges. We nosed through the forest like wolves following scent trails laid out for us. We walked barefoot, stepping lightly, toe-to-heel like foxes, and used our "deer ears" to help locate a beating drum. We identified plants through touch and taste. Many of us even stumbled off to pee somewhere we really hoped was private and not in the vicinity of stinging nettle.

There were expected difficulties – a hawthorn spine in the hand or a trailing blackberry vine wrapped around an ankle like a tripwire. And there were unexpected ones. My awkward self-consciousness, still front and center, even in a group of blinded peers doing exactly the same things I was.

I'm supposed to choose an animal and behave like it? Well that's just ridiculous. (but nobody can see you) But I feel like a fool! I'm an adult human and should act like it. (right, because acting human comes so easily)

I chose a quiet animal, a moth, and flapped my hands a little, head down and flush-faced, away from the action. If any of the raucous squirrels, wildcats, eagles, or bears strayed too near I fluttered the other direction. It was not unlike my experience at the eighth-grade semi-formal. Or a friend's wedding reception I attended last week.

That day, comfortable or not, we all discovered new dimensions of subjects we were studying: animal tracking, bird language, ethnobotany, wilderness survival, and sensory awareness. As we practiced the core routines of Wilderness Awareness School while blindfolded, we were forced to learn not with our eyes but with our whole bodies.

Near the end of the day we were sent off in separate directions to find a place to sit by ourselves – a "sit spot" – to tune in to each sense, one after the other.

I listened to the *chip chip* alarm call of a Pacific wren close by and the spiraling flute-like song of a Swainson's thrush in the distance. I smelled decaying bigleaf maple leaves and mud drying from the morning drizzle. I nibbled the tangy new growth of the hemlock branch angling down to my left. I felt the solid support of the hemlock's trunk at my back and the softer duff of the soil below me.

That was my favorite part of wilderness school, the time allotted for sitting still and paying attention. Alone. It was the only time I felt wholly and consciously at home in my body. If only I got to do that in grade school. If only we all did.

All of us, occasionally, have experiences that are deeply

validating, feed exactly who we are and who we are in the process of becoming. Experiences that answer the question *Who am I on this earth*? Maybe, for some, this first happened within the cinderblock walls of a science room, or English room, on the soccer field or even gym-turned-dance floor. For others, it was between the covers of *The Hobbit* read in a vinyl beanbag chair, through a Led Zeppelin tape played on repeat in the boombox, on the peak of a remote mountain, or on a well-worn animal trail.

If we are lucky enough to recognize what feeds us and can seek out these experiences, we may find them organized into a structured curriculum in a place called a school. More often, though, we discover them quite by happenstance in the school of life. Either way, the journeys might lead us blind and stumbling through the forest. But that isn't necessarily a bad thing.

At the end of the day when our instructors howled and I could finally pull off my blindfold and use my eyes again, I found them changed. Enhanced. I looked out from my body with a soft vision that allowed me to take in the whole three hundred and sixty degree world above, below and around me, all at once. The school calls this "owl eyes."

Every detail of the forest sang its brilliance in shimmering colors and textures, from the luminescent sunlight on moss-draped vine maples and the brilliant yellow flash of the golden-crowned kinglet diving to cover in an emerald sword fern, to the dark place where the cinnamon-red bark of the base of a cedar reached roots down deep into the earth below. I could see that everything around me was vibrantly alive, and that I was a part of it. I also understood that somehow all the loneliness, confusion, and anger that came before were necessary to get me here.

Had I experienced this aliveness, this connectedness before? I had. Would I again? I hoped so. Could I hold on to it, live in it always? I knew by then, I couldn't. But I would do my best to rediscover it. To *dis*-cover: uncover, reveal something hidden, make something new again. As any toddler playing peekaboo would attest, if she could, the moment of discovery is the best part. It doesn't matter that we know what we might find.

There are countless ways to be a human animal, belonging to the earth. Whether you climb mountains, teach children, run marathons, grow vegetables, make art, fight against human injustices, or struggle quietly with your own demons. Whatever your journey, those times in life when a mask falls away and everything makes sense, even if just for a moment, you pay attention. Sometimes they involve an actual blindfold.

Nocturne

Headlights crept round the gravel campground loop toward me, so I slunk behind a cedar and crouched down. In black fleece pants and grey wool jacket with the hood up, clutching my lump of navy-blue sleeping bag, I hoped I'd faded into the dark forest, invisible. No moon illuminated the overcast April sky, so as long as I stayed beyond reach of the headlights, I'd cast no shadow.

~

I used to be scared of the dark. When I was five, monsters lived in my closet – nondescript, unoriginal, generic monsters – and alligators lurked under my bed, inexplicably in the Connecticut suburbs. I never saw them, but I knew they were there in the darkness as surely as the wooden crates of stuffed animals and Matchbox cars. I knew by the way my skin prickled and my throat dried up. I needed to be safe under the covers when Mom turned the light off. If I had to get up later to pee, I'd turn on the bedside light first. Never mind the sleeping sister next to me; she was useless. Alligators waited to sink needled teeth into my bare ankles and monsters waited to seize me with icy fingers and drag me into oblivion. Only light made them disappear.

The logic of adolescence transformed my monsters and alligators into malevolent ghosts and psycho killers. They too tended to hide in my closet and under my bed, the darkest of dark places. In the new, bigger house where we got our own rooms, sometimes I would wake in the night, whether from a crescendo of parental arguing down the hall or from a nightmare, and feel the dread of a hunted animal. An evil presence hovered just above me, its breath on my exposed throat and its bloodshot eyes narrowed to slits, locked on my own. A leaden weight held me down, grew heavier as the seconds ticked on. I'd pull the covers up to my nose and clench my eyes shut, try to reason with myself and fail. Only when I turned the light on would the terror fade. My room was still there: mauve bedspread, purple rug, and ballet-pink walls plastered with black and red band posters: The Cure, The Stone Roses, Social Distortion. Mundane teenage accessories. A little angst, but no evil. I was still there too.

~

The park ranger passed on his evening rounds so I stood and shuffled back to the trail that led away from the campground toward the day-use area. I'd paid for a campsite and set up my tent, but I wasn't going to sleep there that night.

I touched the comforting nylon strap of my headlamp in my pocket but didn't pull it out. I stood still for a few moments, letting my eyes readjust to the blackness. I could smell the rain-soaked earth, fecund with spring nettles, wood ferns, and the luminous white of trillium. A breeze ushered resting raindrops into motion, dripping from centuries-old firs and cedars onto bigleaf maples, down to my face, nose in the air. The saturated wind was loud but not louder than the sound of rushing water in the distance, not louder than my thumping heart. I hugged my sleeping bag to my chest and started walking.

~

Night walks top the lists of both student and staff highlights from residential outdoor schools around the country. As an environmental educator in my twenties, 8 p.m. often found me standing at the front of a line of sixth graders from whichever school was visiting that week, waiting for the nervous squealing and tittering to die down. Once it had, I led them, hands on shoulders or clutching the backpacks of those ahead, away from the nature center and into the New Hampshire night. No city glowed nearby; no streetlight illuminated the dirt road. My red cellophane-covered flashlight was the only source of unnatural light, and I used it sparingly.

From dirt road to trail, I whispered reminders to pick up their feet along the granite rocky path. *Careful of this root. Duck under this branch. Pass it on.* Whenever the kids, being kids, would speak up, laugh loudly, make a ruckus, I would pause. Wait for silence. Refuse to let them fill the night with noise.

In outdoor school, where a walk in the woods is never just a walk in the woods, night walks were interspersed with educational activities. We tested our color vision at night, found it deficient. Assessed our hearing, found it lacking. Smell? Unreliable. Touch? Inadequate. We'd all learned to list the five senses on our five fingers as if they were equal. But fingers aren't equal, and for most of us, sight is the opposable thumb.

After the finale of night walks everywhere, crunching wintergreen Life Savers with mouths open to watch the thrilling chemistry of sugar crystals and wintergreen oil – blue lightning in our mouths – I walked the students back to their dorms.

Then I'd meet up with other instructors to walk the woodland path to our residence, because there was no way in hell I was going to walk that trail alone at night.

~

I'd walked this western Oregon trail dozens of times before, in every season, usually alone. Alone in the woods, I find it easier to stay grounded and present in time and place, to notice and learn more as a naturalist. These days I prefer being alone in general. The older I get the more introverted I become, bordering on reclusive hermit. Around people I'm quick to fatigue, frustrate, even anger. Some days I feel well on my way to being a crazy old cat lady. I just need more cats.

This wood-chipped path through the mixed conifer forest toward the cottonwoods by the Sandy River is my favorite place at Oxbow Park, and one of my favorite places in the natural world. So why was I so uncomfortable there at night? Beyond the workings of an over-active imagination, my throwback to primitive wild hominid predator fears. At night, I was suddenly acutely and disturbingly aware of being alone. A lone animal.

The abrupt weakness or absence of my primary way of connecting with the world handicaps me. That feeling of missing a part of myself leaves me ungrounded, emotionally (and physically) unbalanced. I am less than whole, a shadow of my daytime self.

I sighed, listened for the river, closer now, touched the headlamp in my pocket and kept walking. Tentatively. I picked up my feet to step over obstacles that weren't there.

~

Without flashlights we scattered into the forest, away from each other and off trail, to find a place by ourselves to settle in to our senses. This was the much anticipated 'night sit,' part of the curriculum of Wilderness Awareness School's adult immersion program. Arms waving in front of me, I crashed through shrubs and tripped over logs until I decided I could go no farther and plopped down. I was supposed to tune in to each sense in turn, to ground myself in the forest but only one sense was working that night. Fear.

That wasn't a tame New Hampshire woodland, those were the wild Washington foothills. Cougars lived there! And even if they were few and far between, bobcats and coyotes were common. Wolves were rumored. They say that wild animals are more scared of us than we of them, but I can assure you this wasn't true that night. Nocturnal animals had the clear edge on me, and why shouldn't they seize the opportunity for a weak-eyed, weak-nosed blundering klutz cowering on the cold ground? I was sure my fear broadcast loudly in the night air. Predators prey on weakness.

It's not that I hadn't spent nights outside before, sleeping under the stars in the open air. But I tended to burrow into my bedding before nightfall, then sleep through it. If I left my cocoon for any reason I waved a flashlight ahead of me, erased the dark. Or took other people with me. Safety in numbers.

Knees tucked to my chest, back against a tree, one hour felt like several. Hairs on the back of my neck stood erect. Every stick snap was a beast stalking me, every leaf rustle my impending doom. Some outdoorswoman I was.

Fears may be justified. A night sit would be a bad idea in polar bear country. Or in the middle of an inner-city high crime district for that matter. But was I in real danger that night? Hardly. Monsters and alligators, all over again.

~

It was the witching hour, the time when the veil between worlds is thin, when ghosts appear and walk the earth. Or so they say. But as I arrived at the picnic shelter by the Sandy River I willed my brain to shut up already. Deep breath.

The cottonwood buds, sticky with amber resin, were just starting to leaf out, releasing an intoxicating perfume in the riparian air. Out of the forest by the expansive river I recognized where the muted charcoal sky met black lines of trees and then the kinetic indigo sheen of water. I made my way to the lone fir tree at the end of the grassy knoll before the sloping bouldered riverbank. I would be sheltered there when the soft rain started again. After I removed my boots and tucked into my sleeping bag, back against the solid fir, I breathed easier. That night I would sleep with the river. Or more likely, stay awake.

~

Half our lives, our world turns its face away from the sun. If we always sleep through it or fill it with artificial light and noise, what are we missing? Doesn't the night world feel like more than just the day world without light? Not just in our bedrooms, behind closed doors, but outside. What is this mysterious new place, and who are we here? The rules have changed, but we don't know the new ones.

Maybe it is all in my head. A diurnal animal's fears predicating heightened awareness, alertness, magnified be-here-nowness, all for the sake of survival. But if I am more attentive, more tuned in to my world, what might I notice that I wouldn't in light of day? What lurks among us, just beyond the limits of our weak senses? When we turn up the volume, the intensity, what might we find?

~

I heard rowdy teenagers coming from the campground; their brash voices and explosive laughter reached me long before their beams pierced the blackness. I didn't want their light, their noise. Not that night.

In my forties, I'm still scared of the dark. I still prefer to light it up or sleep through it. But I've come to understand that to truly know the places I love, I must haunt them at night. I want to learn what fear has to teach me, discover what it can show me. I want to glimpse the peculiar, the extraordinary, the mystical lurking in the shadows, not cling to the mundane in the light. Not screw my eyes shut and choose ignorance. I no longer believe in evil or monsters but I do get the feeling that there is more out there than meets the imperfect eye. Maybe one day I'll even be ready to gaze into my own bloodshot eyes and face oblivion.

I squatted on my haunches and crept behind the tree. When the teens arrived and their lights strobed toward the river I moved backward over the lip of the knoll. A rock loosened and tumbled down the bank, an echo and splash. They screamed and I skulked lower. They didn't come closer. They seemed frozen at the head of the trail. When a barred owl barked his hoarse call downriver they'd had enough, and retreated quickly to their campfire. I exhaled a faint chuckle, like a hiss.

Sometimes, I am the beast in the darkness. Sometimes, I am the ghost.

Communion

Jeff closed his eyes, brought the cigarette to his lips and inhaled. He held the smoke in his mouth, curled it into his tongue, swallowed some of it and let the rest swirl away in the morning fog.

"Okay, I'm ready." He stubbed out the cigarette on the bottom of his hiking boot, handed it and the lighter to one of our instructors, pushed up his wire-rimmed glasses and fell in line with the rest of us as we tromped into the forest. Twenty-nine students climbed over mossy logs, pushed through waist-high sword ferns, and crunched sticks underfoot, following our four leaders without question. A disparate gang of eighteen- to sixty-five-year-olds bundled in all manner of torn and patched earth-toned wool and the latest breathable odor-free synthetic long underwear and Gore-Tex, we carried no backpacks, no water bottles, no trail mix. We held nothing in our pockets – no matches, no knives. We didn't know our destination, only that we would remain there for five days with just the clothes on our backs. Though my stomach still digested eggs scrambled with kale, onion and goat cheese, it growled expectantly. I reminded myself, *You chose this.*

Survival week was a much-anticipated culminating rite of passage of Wilderness Awareness School's adult immersion program. I had signed up for the nine-month program because as a native New Englander, I wanted to connect more deeply with the landscape of my chosen home in the West. As an environmental educator, I wanted to gain additional experience and make connections to improve my job prospects in the field. As a summer-camp-raised school lover, I was drawn to an adult outdoor school that sounded like camp. And as a truth seeking, spiritually curious, wandering thirty-four-year-old, I was searching for enlightenment through communion with nature. Yes, that's all.

The program had delivered on all counts, even brief instances of total clarity and oneness with everything. The five days of true wilderness immersion looked to be the deepest experience yet. I was finally going to become my wild self and learn what it had to teach me.

It was early May in the foothills of the Washington Cascades but February's frosty breath lingered. A low, saturated cloud dripped from Douglas firs and western redcedars, which as we walked gave way to the naked limbs of bigleaf maples, red alders, and cottonwoods. The air grew thicker, soupier. What the changing landscape suggested, my ears confirmed. We approached a swollen river. Minutes later we arrived at the smooth-stoned edge of the tumultuous river, raging with snowmelt.

"This is where we say goodbye," our instructor, Chris, said.

"Here?" Caroline asked. She tucked a lock of gray hair back under a gray wool hat and cinched the strings of her green camo sweatshirt tighter around her throat.

"Nope." Chris turned and pointed across the river. I squinted toward the far shore and saw the river split and disappear behind forested land, then merge again downriver. An island. "There," he said.

Let the communing begin.

Another instructor, Angie, lifted a handmade drum from her bag and beat a rhythm as she, Chris, Marcus, and Alexia sang a ceremonial send-off. The river roared an accompaniment. With varying degrees of modesty and self-consciousness, we disrobed to underwear or other minimal layers and bundled loose clothes and shoes around our shoulders. In twos and threes, we strode into the icy river. Step by step, facing into the current, we struggled to find steady footing while holding on to our dry clothes and each other. In four steps the water was up to my waist. The river pushed and churned around me, but I felt strong. *Bring it on.*

Soon twenty-nine people dripped, shivered, and shimmied on one shore as we beseeched numb fingers to tug on pants and boots, zip sweatshirts and button flies. Our four teachers, now tiny in the distance of the other shore, abruptly stopped singing and disappeared into the forest. The river roared.

We knew what we had to do. With so many adults of various ages and backgrounds, we were not exactly an efficient, utilitarian beehive. But after nine months of learning survival skills and each other, we were also not likely to become *Lord of the Flies* savages. With little discussion, we got to work.

What presumably had been a peaceful woodland became a flurry of activity and discordance. Our best friction fire-makers scavenged for materials and soon huffed and puffed over the hand-drill or bow-drill techniques, a squeaky screech of cedar on cedar that silenced birds and competed with the river music.

Others crashed through the forest in search of a safe water source or hunted for the green stuff that would start our food cache: salmonberry shoots, Siberian miner's lettuce, stinging nettles, dandelion greens, broad-leaved plantain, red dock, sheep sorrel, and other early spring leaves. The rest of us agreed on a central camp area and bustled like beavers as we dragged dead branches and gathered insulation materials for shelters. Though many of us would typically *take only pictures, leave only footprints*, when you're damp, chilled, and facing five days on a riparian islet in a rainforest, you revise your priorities.

By the time shadows gathered into twilight, our makeshift village boasted multiple-occupancy and solo shelters, round yurt-like forts and open-ended lean-tos. Some of us tucked up near the fire ring where hemlock and cedar smoked and hissed, others off in the woods away from everyone. For the extra challenge I chose a spot off to the side and built my own stick-framed lean-to layered with bigleaf maple and Japanese knotweed leaves over a bed of hemlock needles.

With shelter, fire, food, and a clear seep of water nearby, we were prepared for a relaxed week. The anxious knot I hadn't noticed lodged in my abdomen began to unravel, leaving only a clean, uncomplicated pang of hunger. No problem. There was plenty to eat and I had nothing but time. Time to forage for food, feed the fire, contemplate my life, and be wild.

I gathered with some of the others by the fire. We sang folk songs and chuckled about our grumbling stomachs. Eighteen-year-old Lily told jokes and laughed her big, contagious belly laughs. Then the rain returned and most of us retired to our shelters.

I crawled into my lean-to and lay on my back in all my clothes – long underwear, wool layers, rain gear, and heavy boots. Raindrops patted and plopped. I shuddered in the raw air, saturated hemlock needles below and decaying leaves inches from my face above. I blinked in the darkness. The ground felt hard as concrete and a root jabbed my hip. I wondered how bears spend a winter like this, whether they too know claustrophobia.

I tried to ignore the discomfort and be grateful. I was safe, healthy, and all my basic needs were met. Wasn't I lucky, to have this experience that few Westerners would? I breathed the moist air. I listened to the river in the distance, the crackle of the fire a little closer. I waited.

After several hours my eyes finally drooped shut and I nearly fell into a dream when a sound jolted me awake. Louder than the rain. Closer. Leaves shifted, something rustled. Snapped. Crunched.

Beetles? Termites? Mice? An over-active imagination? I glowered at the blackness as my heart pulsed. The cold. The hard ground. The critters. The earthen walls closing in around me.

I gave up on sleep and the challenge of going it alone, wriggled out of my shelter and moved toward the light of the fire.

A few others lay there, feeding the flames from the cache nearby. The fire was hot enough by then that it didn't matter that the wood was wet though it sizzled and sputtered as it burned. I wormed my way between cigarette-starved Jeff and peacefully snoozing Lily and listed so close to the blaze that my wet clothes were soon steaming. Warmer then, I lay on my side. I dozed off for a few minutes, then flipped over to warm the cold wet side and cool the dry burning side. Five of us spent the first night like that, slumped against each other like a pack of restless hounds.

Night faded into day. I had barely slept at all. Bleary-eyed, I watched the fire flicker and listened to the birds wake up. The constant river had faded to white noise. Rain dripped off the cedars above onto our faces, flushed with fire. In my exhaustion my community members began to fade too, both extensions of myself and just other animals who inhabited the woods with me. Two of us swatted simultaneously at the smoking hat of a woman sleeping too close to the flames. She grunted and turned over.

I was fading into my animal self.

I rubbed at the sting of smoke in my eyes and trudged to the watering hole where I splayed on my belly and lowered my head to drink. Crawling a few feet away, I munched some miner's lettuce. My stomach grumbled dissent.

Some others were going exploring and I decided to join them. As we traversed the shoreline of the island we found an assortment of items that had washed up in high water. A barbeque grate, a metal frying pan, empty soda bottles. With our plunder we could cook over the fire instead of in it and carry water away from the seep. I found a bottle that once held grape soda and didn't think about germs, just how great it would be to guzzle from a bottle instead of lapping from a trickle. I was thirsty.

We tried to walk the circumference of the island but the rocky shoreline and dense tangled undergrowth meant constant zig-zagging in and out of an already jagged perimeter. The island was bigger than we'd thought and soon we were lost. When we finally found our way back to the village the sun had moved across the sky and we were shaken, scratched bloody from blackberry and salmonberry thorns, and exponentially more hungry and thirsty. We beelined to the water seep.

We should never have wandered so far. That was fucking stupid, wasting so much energy, Caroline snarled, eyes flaring. Hunger and anxiety had provoked one of the most even-tempered to bare her claws. I bit my tongue.

I filled my bottle, gulped grape-flavored water, filled it again, and vowed never to venture so far from the village. I returned to my shelter, considered a nap. I kneeled on wet ground and peered into the dank cave, shivered, and stood up again. Looked through the trees toward the fire. Who was I kidding? I grabbed the main support branch and yanked it out, collapsing the structure. Then, dragging the log behind me, I returned to the fire, tossed it in, and curled up next to it.

What happened to my love of solitude? Did my self-sufficient independent spirit have limits? Was I slinking back to community or physical comfort? Or were the two intertwined more than I cared to admit?

If I had to survive alone, Robinson Crusoe-style, I probably could. But would I choose that? Hell no. I couldn't fathom that anyone else would. I prefer Henry David Thoreau's version. A quiet cabin on the outskirts of a friendly town. With guests, sometimes. But I was starting to realize that just living simply, even deliberately, is not going wild.

I awoke to darkness. The number of fire sleepers had grown from the five the first night, but leveled out to a comfortable and variable eight to ten for the rest of the week. The others had faded into the forest and only appeared now and then to check in. Our continually fed bonfire allowed ample space for those present to lie down or lean on each other to nap. Nobody seemed to sleep soundly, so as a group we managed to feed the flames and keep each other from burning up.

When the sun rose again I thought I would take a short wander on my own, to find solitude and perhaps some clarity away from the others. When I stood, the world went black and I staggered on wobbly knees. Hunger and lack of sleep left me weaker than I'd expected. Determined, I stumbled away anyway. I found I had to lean against a tree or sit down after every twenty feet or so. Stumble stumble stumble – lean – stumble stumble stumble – plop down.

I found a cedar by the river and slouched against it. As I gazed at the shore in the distance I felt none of the peace and contentment I usually did during a quiet woodland sit. Wasn't this beautiful? Wasn't I blessed to be here? Was I one with nature? What's nature? I tried to contemplate my life and came up with nothing. Not joy, or sadness, not one deep thought, just... nothing.

And then...

I'm hungry. I looked down, picked some violet leaves and chewed listlessly. My stomach churned.

If this was enlightenment I wasn't sure I wanted it anymore. Maybe this is what it really meant to be wild, to inhabit animal skin. To step off the human roller coaster to the realm of equanimity. No misery, no ecstasy. I never thought I'd say this, but I prefer humanity.

The rest of the week I stuck to the fire. Though I was painfully hungry, my stomach turned at the thought of putting anything else green and fibrous in my mouth. When I managed to muster the saliva and jaw muscles necessary to get the stuff down, I ended up hungrier than before. It just wasn't worth it. So I stopped eating. I only got up to refill my water bottle and to pee, though neither of those things were necessary very often anymore. As for the other bathroom question, my large intestine seemed to have shut down entirely for lack of anything to process. I didn't have to go dig a hole once the whole five days. Problem solved.

This wasn't the communion I'd expected. For the handful of us who stayed with the fire day and night there was only commiserating. And we weren't restless dogs anymore. We were edgy wolverines.

"I want a cigarette," Jeff growled about once an hour.

"I'd kill for a cup of hot coffee," Matt muttered.

"I'll pay you to cross the river and bring back a pizza," Khy pleaded.

Our cravings elicited hours of almost philosophical discussions about what we wanted and how we wanted it. New York bagel with lox and cream cheese. Linguini with Alfredo sauce. Hamburger, extra rare, with smoked gouda, avocado and onions. Salmon baked in butter and garlic. We formed epic eating plans as we salivated and turned up our noses at the greenery available to us. Like a many-headed monster of insatiable desire, we fed the fire and fanned the flames of our discontent.

I knew that others were having different experiences on that island. And that it had nothing to do with preparations or skills-knowledge, but something deeper. I understood that, and though part of me felt like a failure, I also felt powerless to do a single thing about it.

One of the others brought a garter snake to the fire, skinned it, roasted it, and passed it around. Another brought a baby robin and cooked it on a glowing ember. We smacked our lips at these delicacies and forced ourselves to share with the other fire tenders. Snake and robin were the most delectable things I ate on that island, and if I had the energy, I'd have gone out and found some more. Yes, even sweet little baby birds right out of the nest. In the real world I am an obsessive bird-lover, but on that island I would have broken their necks without a second thought. *That* is hunger.

I'd become a savage after all.

The last night was the longest. Not having slept at all, we fire tenders disassembled the village long before the first robin's *cheep tut tut tut.* Slowly, those we'd barely seen all week filtered back toward camp and helped us extinguish our five-day fire.

We circled up around smoldering embers and sang a song of gratitude. As we sang, three adult blacktail deer walked out of the woods and continued toward us. They were the first, the only deer we'd seen all week. They stopped within fifteen feet of our circle and watched us, black tails twitching, bronze bodies still. Six ears panned our way. We kept singing.

Were they blessing us? Had we proven ourselves? Or were they saying, *Good riddance clumsy humans, you've lost what you once had?*

Tears blurred my vision as I watched the animals watch us.

One of them blinked, lush eyelashes momentarily obscuring obsidian eyes. Otherwise, the deer remained still. We were still, too.

In the deer's gaze I felt my self-criticism drain away. Left in its place – serene joy and intense gratitude. Only when we finished our song did the deer stroll around us and off into the green. We watched them until they disappeared.

It was the closest I came all week to communing with nature. The rest of the time I was too busy inhabiting my body. Feeling hunger, thirst, cold, and fatigue as only an animal can, and the discomfort of yearning as only a human can. How challenging, how confusing, how painful to be both! What a surprise to realize that I wouldn't have it any other way. Maybe that was all my wild self had to teach me, and maybe that was enough.

Time to go. We walked through the woods back to the river-crossing spot and only had to wait a few minutes for Chris, Angie, Marcus, and Alexia to appear out of the trees on the other side. When we heard them start to sing, we knew we were allowed to return.

We all survived, in our own ways, and we were going home. To a bottomless well of clean, clear water. To the most mouthwatering, satisfying meal I would ever taste. To the miracles of hot showers, walls that keep the heat in and the wet out, and a big soft bed that was all mine. To all the physical comforts that free our minds to wonder, contemplate, and dream. It was not the enlightenment I had expected, but a rare and precious gift nonetheless.

Twenty-nine leaner, lighter, clear-eyed people crossed that river again and rejoined the four on the other shore. Though as the saying goes, you never step in the same river twice.

Speaking Bird

From where I stood near the grassy pinnacle of East Portland's Mt. Tabor I could see only the bird's head, but I clearly identified the black mask, yellow face, and insect-eating beak of a Townsend's warbler. My survey partners a few feet away, however, saw its slate-colored back and white belly and named it a hermit warbler.

"Hermits don't have black masks," I insisted, pointing at the picture in my Sibley guide.

"Townsend's don't have grey backs and unstreaked flanks," the silver-haired husband-wife team countered, pointing at the other bird's picture on the same page.

Finally, when the bird in question moved into clear view on a bigleaf maple branch, we understood. The bird was both species, or neither. A hybrid, or hermit/Townsend's cross. Though this breaks a basic biological rule we learned in grade school – separate species cannot interbreed – some species are so closely related that they can. And do.

Now how the heck would I record this fellow in proper four-letter ornithological code on my datasheet? And when did I become such a nerd?

Rules, naming, cataloguing – none of it made the slightest difference to that bird, of course. Why did I care?

I wasn't an obsessive kid. Like a lot of little girls, I loved horses, had a picture book of horses I loved to stare at and imagined riding, but I never bothered to learn about them. I couldn't name any of the breeds or where they came from. I knew even less about dinosaurs, dogs, racecars, ballerinas, movie stars, baseball cards, or any of the things that occupied my friends. I was always a generalist, never delving into any one thing. I remember a boy in high school who was fascinated by butterflies, who knew everything about them and spewed butterfly facts to anyone who would listen. I didn't understand the big deal about butterflies and I certainly didn't envy him the teasing this spurred, but I did wonder what it might be like to care about one thing so deeply.

~

One March morning I drove across the tracks of industrial Northwest Portland and over the Sauvie Island Bridge to a rural oasis. A neon-orange fireball the size of a grapefruit drizzled sunrise onto the confluence of the Multnomah Channel and Willamette River, but the island was still bathed in shadows. My car crept between towering blackberry brambles and expansive pastures to Wapato State Greenway's gravel parking lot.

Binocular strap heavy on my wool-clad shoulders, clipboard under my arm, I greeted my fellow bird surveyors Pam and Peg with a smile and a nod. We stepped softly into the day, eyes and ears open. In the distance a coyote skulked through dewy almost frosty grass, head barely visible above the silvery green. Lines and V's of waterfowl spanned the sky like worn corduroy, until a low-flying harrier spooked the lake swimmers and the sky darkened with disorganized swarms of them. Canada geese, cackling geese, tundra swans, ducks galore and those squawking modern dinosaurs—sandhill cranes. So much sky filled with so many big birds with so much to say. Honk, cackle, squeak, and croak, a riotous discordance.

But we were there to attend to smaller melodies. Arriving at our first counting station, I readied my clipboard and pencil and counted down one minute of waiting, until...*Go.* My companions and mentors, the counters, rattled off bird names and I scribbled codes as fast as cold fingers could move.

Black-capped chickadee, Anna's hummingbird, spotted towhee, ruby-crowned kinglet, brown creeper, and on and on until pausing, heads cocked, a question and answer session: *Did you hear...? Was that a...? Did we get a...? How many of those do we have?* and finally a click of the stopwatch and my *Done.*

We relaxed into easy conversation as we slogged the muddy path to the next counting station, then repeated the count in the waxing light. We continued this routine for eight points on the two-mile loop through forest and field, around marsh and pond. Pam, a kind, contemplative woman of my mother's generation, and Peg, closer to grandmother with warm hugs and effusiveness to match, were always a joy to be around whether the birds were flying or not.

Though our quiet morning ritual may have been special to us, we could have been poster children for birders. We three middle-aged and older, educated, Caucasian women are the exact demographic of the majority of North American birders. And as of 2016, according to a U.S. Fish and Wildlife Service report on birding in the United States, there are more than forty-five million of us. That's almost fifteen percent of the U.S. population.

Though I understand that natural resource inventories are important to the scientific community, to add to our knowledge and monitor the health of various ecosystems, I don't survey birds in the name of science. Few of the forty-five million birders do. It's personal. There is something we're hungry for, something that feeds us in the ability to name the feathered earthlings, to know the particular type of warbler sharing a hilltop with us or the various species in a mixed flock gleaning insects by a wetland. The more we name, the more we may be driven to understand their particular life histories, their idiosyncratic behaviors, beyond the simple concept of *bird* or even *warbler.*

Naming evokes familiarity. Spying a Townsend's (or hermit) warbler in the pond-side willow tree now sends the sort of joyful sparks to my brain and heart that say *friend.* The more birds named, the more friends surround me. And birds are most everywhere. But so are insects, and if you're lucky, trees, grasses, and wildflowers. Why birds?

For some of us, they are just easy to see. Birds are flashy, often beautifully colorful, animated, just the right size to spot and watch for a while, and busy enough to keep us engaged. Or maybe they stimulate our brains, fire the synapses of questioning and puzzling, then after a confident identification or behavioral discovery, the satisfaction of a complex riddle solved. For others, birding is serious competition. With adequate study, enough time, and the right equipment, most anyone with keen sight and/or hearing can compete for most bird species or individuals in a given region or time period. Who doesn't want to be a winner? For all these reasons and more, the U.S. Fish and Wildlife Service reports that in 2011, Americans spent upwards of $14 billion on birding trips and $26 billion on wildlife-watching equipment and supplies. That's a lot of binoculars, bird baths, and bird seed.

Also? Maybe birds are my speed. My mind flits around, darts and dives and twitches at times, and other times perches immobile, faintly ruffling in the breeze.

I do know that the more I pay attention to my feathered

friends, the more they teach me about my home. On Sauvie Island we learned which types of trees host the red-bellied sapsuckers, and that a thick clump of pendulous moss just might be a bushtit nest. We discovered that European starlings can convincingly mimic bald eagle cries, but that the robins' high-pitched alarm calls alert us to the location of the real eagles.

In learning the lessons of one place, we can become more fluent in the language of other places. Now when I see a cottonwood tree, I look for the telltale geometric designs of the sapsucker. When I see a clump of moss, I look closer, and listen. When I notice a group of starlings in downtown Portland or Seattle I might hear in their repertoire hints of barking dogs and car alarms. And when I discern that same high-pitched call from robins in a city park I might look up to discover a barred owl hidden high in a Douglas fir. My cognizance of birds is teaching me the language of my entire landscape.

Maybe it was the ornithology class in graduate school followed by a season as a hawk researcher and an internship with a bird zoo that put me over the edge. Facilitated learning and intimate connections that turned a generalist naturalist into bird nerd, or "twitterhead" as a friend dubbed me, back when the word twitter still referred to bird sounds. It's developed slowly; I'm still no expert and I don't need to be. But yes, I am fascinated, ravenous for new bird knowledge and experiences and will indeed spew bird facts to anyone who will listen. When I see the polite smile and placating nod of a friend to whom I've just gushed about watching a female red-naped sapsucker interacting congenially with a male red-breasted sapsucker, with whom they sometimes hybridize, I realize I've arrived. Like butterfly boy, I'm a fanatic.

~

In another wild greenway southwest of Portland, Tryon Creek

State Park, I joined a night survey. Nighttime in the forest has its own lessons to teach. Seeing moves into the background as other senses wake up. Smells seem stronger – the organic odors of decaying leaves, moss, and mushrooms mingled with clay silt and basalt from the canyon bottom. The meandering stream that was barely audible in the daylight a few hours before sounded like a whitewater river, announcing "water here" to thirsty creatures of the night.

My team of five – Mary, Candace, Sarah, Casey, and I – moved away from the dim lights of the nature center into the blackness of the Big Fir Trail. We stopped and blinked, willing night vision to kick in quickly. Feeling the trail beneath our feet, we let muscle memory tell us where to go. We didn't speak but focused all our energy on listening. We were straining to hear sounds behind our shuffling footsteps, beyond the insistent creek. We were listening for owls.

At our first checkpoint, I drew in my breath and paused as I first mentally practiced the short whistled call and then: "who... who.... who-who-who-whoowhoowhoowhoowhoo," the rhythm of a ping-pong ball dropped on a table and bouncing to stillness. Though I'd practiced this call for weeks I wondered if it was good enough to either fool the western screech owl or at least spark its curiosity enough to beckon it closer. Or any other owl for that matter. The official purpose of our research was to document numbers and locations of owls in the park. Unofficially, we were a flock of new and old friends bound by a common passion.

We each find our own ways of opening doors to the world around us. For those of us entranced by the natural world, there are countless ways in. Gardening, animal tracking, rock climbing, fly-fishing, trail running. Birding may not have called to me from the beginning, and maybe I just happened to wander in that oft-opened door, but I'm so glad I stuck around.

Silence. Trees whispered, the creek mumbled and hissed, a

branch fell to the forest floor a few yards away, and silence. I wondered if anyone else had forgotten to breathe. I turned one hundred and eighty degrees and called again: "Who... who.... who-who-who-whoowhoowhoowhoowhoo." If they were listening, they did not answer.

Just then a fire engine screamed down the street adjacent to the park, leaving in its wake an even louder silence and then, just as suddenly, the yippings and yowlings of a pack of coyotes. The noise seemed to come from all around us, and we instinctively drew closer together until the primal din quieted. Mary, Sarah and I stifled giggles. Candace whispered *Wow.* Stoic Casey exhaled. We continued up the trail to the next point.

Just as Candace began the whistled call, we heard it. She froze with pursed lips. Hands cupped around ears and heads tilted we strained to stretch our mediocre human hearing out into the night. "Toot-toot-toot-toot-toot-toot..." the steady rhythmic whistling reached us from the darkness to the north. I pointed, and noticed my teammates were pointing the same direction. Our ears agreed. With improving night vision I saw the shining eyes of my fellow owlers as we whispered and nodded our agreement. "Saw-whet!"

I penciled on the data sheet: NSWO (Northern Saw Whet Owl). Once named, we knew that somewhere out there was a robin-sized little owl with brown stripes and bright yellow eyes. A bird we learned about in our books, but also knew personally from previous nights in the park. That little owl with a call as steady as my heartbeat was telling anyone who would listen, "I am here."

We were listening. We're listening still.

Bodhi Tree

I. The Detective

With sapphire eyes blazing above a gnome-like salt and pepper beard, Professor Tom Wessels perched on the corner of a desk at the head of the classroom. He drummed his fingertips together with palms cupped open as if cradling a crystal ball, and he asked us questions. One day it might be "Why are there so many stone walls running through the middle of our forests?" The next, "How might you know whether a forest has experienced a major hurricane? And when? And which direction did it move through?" "What does a forest full of multi-trunked hardwoods and pitch pines suggest?" "How about a few scattered 'wolf trees'?"

Like a two-year-old fascinated with a mysterious world, he implored his graduate students, day after day, why? How come? How do you know? He knew the answers, but that didn't take the edge off his contagious excitement, nor was he tempted to rob us of our own discoveries. In this basic Principles of Ecology class where one might expect lectures droning terms and concepts like 'carrying capacity' and 'disturbance regime,' I regularly heard the kinds of curious questions that made me sit up straight and think *Wait a minute, you can know that? You can learn how to tell that? Why didn't I ever think about that before?*

Tom explains in his book *Reading the Forested Landscape:*

> Whenever I encounter a change in the composition of the forest, such as a dense stand of hemlock abutting an older stand of beech and sugar maple, I am compelled to solve the mystery: What created this change in vegetation? ... To people not as experienced in the process of 'reading the landscape,' I might appear somewhat like Holmes through Watson's eyes. Yet this process is not as difficult as it seems. It demands only some new observational skills – and knowledge about the kinds of clues to look for.

The most basic principles of ecology, he taught us, are the capacity for observation and the curiosity to wonder, W*hy?*

We did have a textbook, though I don't recall a thing about it. After the questions came not lectures, but deeper inquiries, investigations. Theoretical discussions in our classroom of the Antioch University New England campus or, whenever he could manage to get us outside into the feral adjacent lot or a nearby woodland, experiential lessons we could learn with our bodies.

"What do you notice about the age of this forest?" he'd prod us, and after we'd recognize the contrast of a tall, mature overstory with lush, young understory and few middle-aged trees, he'd have us scrambling for other clues. We dug in the soil, peered closely at a black scar on a tree here, a silvery hue to a snag there, and then *Voila!* A forest fire, revealed.

We would eventually come to the terms and concepts, the scientific language of ecology, but always organically within our explorations. In learning to read the natural world with Tom

Wessels, I felt less like a scientist and more like an adventurer, a magician reaching into a black hat and pulling out a rabbit. Kids naturally step into such roles. But adult students working toward a master of science degree? That is the work of a great teacher.

I've been blessed with a multitude of great teachers in my life, which may have something to do with why I keep going back to school. I had other excellent teachers at Antioch. But there was something about Tom Wessels that was more than a great teacher, something that made me want to follow him around or sit at his feet, waiting for enlightenment.

In our small, community-focused graduate school I felt I knew him fairly well, but we were never close. Not the warm, effusive, extroverted sort, Tom's quiet, Buddha-like composure as he waited in silence for his class to think about a question he'd posed could be unsettling. "What can you learn from a series of flat-topped stumps in a hemlock forest?"

Who cares about stumps, you ask? If you'd been in that class with the pointy-bearded professor wielding the invisible crystal ball, if you'd glimpsed the gears turning behind those glacial blue eyes, I assure you, you would care. When he lasered those eyes my direction it was all I could do to stutter a weak attempt at an intelligent reply. "It was logged?"

A faint nod, fingertips drumming, eyes beaming around the room. "Yes. But what else?"

He wasn't demanding or critical. But he knew things, everything it seemed, and in his presence I became the shy little girl who knew nothing. But after he'd given more clues and patiently teased the answers from us, we too knew how those unassuming stumps could point to when the logging happened, how many times, what species were cut, and why.

Rather than intimidate me into apathy, Tom's teaching felt like an invitation. We could know the answers too. We could read natural landscapes too. We could be like him.

As a lucky participant of a Sonoran Desert ecology field-study trip, I and a dozen other master's and Ph.D. students got to spend ten days frolicking in remote backcountry Baja, California, with Tom. Spending the days traversing red rock hills, sandy beaches, cholla and ocotillo lowlands and palo verde highlands, we put Tom's teaching philosophy into practice. Running breathless back to camp or huddled around the campfire at night we'd demand, *What's this? How come? What about that? Why? Why? Why?*

He listened attentively, nodding. He knew the answers. Or he didn't. Or we figured them out together. Or we didn't. But we were learning that the answers were not nearly as important as the questions.

I may not remember much of what I learned about the Sonoran Desert, but I can still feel the excitement of inquiry, the fulfillment of exploring the arid landscape. The hollow, sun-bleached bone that sits on my windowsill today, the one we discovered was a pelican femur, has less to do with the factual knowledge of pelicans and more to do with a deep, visceral intimacy with an ecosystem, the feeling of sitting sun-burned and squinting on baking sand, watching a white pelican circle and then dive, missile-like, deep into a cerulean sea to emerge with a fish.

You might argue that I'd already been passionate about nature, having enrolled in a master's program in environmental biology. I had considered myself an environmentalist from a young age, had already worked as an environmental educator and knew some natural history – the names of some trees and flowers and birds and frogs. But I wouldn't say I was a true naturalist, a passionate student of ecology, not until graduate school. Not until Tom Wessels. Tom's gift as a teacher was the wide-eyed, gape-mouthed, gleeful awe of nature that only comes with intimate knowledge of the interconnected webs of whole landscapes. So much more than a mass of individuals sharing space, ecology reveals the complex, complicated, sometimes fantastically surprising relationships among them. By turning me into a questioning ecologist, Tom helped me begin to glimpse the beautiful, mysterious intricacy of our world, and where I fit.

II. The Mystic

Chris Laliberte hopped from one leg to another, spritely as a wood nymph despite his heavy frame. He was just getting going. A cedar fire snapped in the center of the earthen-floored hut as he tugged at his shaggy shoulder-length hair, gesticulated, paced, and orated without taking a breath.

He could have been talking wildlife tracking, friction fire-making, ethnobotany or sneaky stalking skills. Or some of the more theoretical aspects of Wilderness Awareness School's curriculum like cognitive theories of awareness, methods of nature mentoring, or the sociological importance of rites of passage. But regardless of the subject matter, our cohort of thirty adults was in for an engaging ride when Chris was teaching.

I chose the nine-month program as a crash course in Pacific Northwest natural history, a bridge between the master of science I'd gained in the Northeast and my ecologically distinct home in the Northwest. I thought this field-based certificate program in the foothills of Washington's Cascades might be more fun than going back to traditional school and yet still might land me a job as a naturalist. But on day one, when Chris stood before us and started giving thanks to the birds, the plants, the fish, the waters, and on and on until he'd covered just about everything including sun, moon, and stars, I understood that the program was going to be more than natural history and fun.

I wasn't raised with religion and tend to bristle at most spiritual talk. In my life I'd wavered from atheist to agnostic to *Who the hell knows—I'm an ecologist.* But there was someone in front of me spouting that woo-woo mindfulness stuff and it wasn't shutting me down. What was going on?

It could be that I knew he was a scientifically educated naturalist, an environmental educator like me, as well as a Ph.D. candidate in mythological studies. I respected him as an academic, despite the fact that he'd just said, "I would like to bring our attention to all the four-legged animals, especially to Trickster Coyote, and send out thanks for them."

Or maybe it was because he was talking about stuff that just made sense to me, that fit in with my growing awareness of and gleeful joy in all that is not human in the world. I *was* thankful for the birds and trees and waters and coyotes. Chris wasn't asking us to be thankful *to* anyone in particular. Gratitude was the point, and I felt it. Starting the day with this "Thanksgiving Address" gifted to the school by a Haudenosaunee elder grounded me somehow, opened my mind and my heart at the same time. So by the time the grinning mad-scientist in front of me moved from earth to sky to outer space and landed on "the spirit that moves through all things," I was still nodding in agreement.

This wasn't Chris' personal philosophy but the philosophy of the school, a school founded on a mosaic of global indigenous teachings and practices to facilitate deep nature connection. A school that employs other excellent teachers. But there was something about Chris in particular, something that made me want to follow him around or sit at his feet, waiting for enlightenment. In the spirit of Tom's teaching philosophy, I subverted my introvert nature and reached out to Chris in an attempt to explore the mystery of *why*?

In questioning the intersection of nature and spirituality, I learned that for Chris, nature connection *is* his spirituality. "I don't care about the underlying truth of whether there's *really* another being there relating to me when I have an interaction with a rock, I'm happy to just admit that we'll probably never figure out how to determine that. But I'm also happy to say that it feels better, more satisfying, more interesting, to play along and say 'Yeah, that rock really did call out to me—it intentionally caught my attention, amidst the whole carpet of random rocks. *This* one is trying to engage me in a conversation. What's up, rock?' Why the hell not?"

You can be an academic AND talk to rocks? Sign me up! Chris was a role model for how an emotional connection and open-mindedness to the mysteries of the natural world could coexist in a logical mind. A mind that can be equally fascinated by learning the three different varieties of chemicals in stinging nettle and how they act on the human body. Spirit and nature, as one.

Like Tom Wessels, Chris Laliberte also believed in the power of story. He had plenty of his own, but in wilderness school he sometimes read to us, shared some of his favorite stories by others. The story I remember clearest is by Ursula LeGuin, titled "Buffalo Gals, Won't You Come Out Tonight."

As the mist dripped down green vine maples onto moss and sword ferns outside our shelter, as we stoked the fire and settled in on wooden benches or the earthen floor for the oldest human means of communicating, Chris read LeGuin's magical mystical tale. In it, a young girl falls from a plane, survives, and lives for a time in the company of a coyote and a village of other animals, all of whom the girl can understand and sees as somewhat odd humans. Through the girl's new eyes we see the human world from the animals' perspective, all the noise and chaos and busyness, as well as the wastefulness and cruelty, culminating in her adopted momma coyote being purposefully poisoned. In the end the girl must face up to who she is and return to her people. As she resists leaving, she hears a final message, "'Go on, little one, Granddaughter,' Spider said. 'Don't be afraid. You can live well there. I'll be there too, you know. In your dreams, in your ideas, in dark corners in the basement.'"

Despite having read this story many times over the years, Chris choked up. It was my first time hearing it and the tears flowed freely. What was it about this story that so deeply affected us? It seemed as if LeGuin spoke directly to me, someone who found such deep kinship with the natural world that the human one often felt foreign, even cruel. I, too, often wanted to run off and live in that animal village, forever. Watching Chris similarly moved by the story, I imagined he felt the same.

Maybe the underlying reason for my idolization of teachers like Tom Wessels and Chris Laliberte was the feeling that they experienced the world similarly, that they moved through the world as I did. They may have figured out how to do it better, with more grace, perhaps, and definitely more wisdom. But maybe the point is not that I wanted to be like them, but that in the deepest parts of my psyche I already was.

Chris explained, "Nature connection is my reality check. I find it very calming—it helps me deal with chronic stress and anxiety due to the expectations and requirements of social and professional relations. Just getting nature-time gives me a visceral reassurance that yes, there's something solid, real, and sensible underlying all the crap that humans have decided is *so important* that we have to arrange our lives and our behavior and actions around it. I can feel what's real and remember that all that social stuff is just a game, and I can once again play the game because I choose to."

During class, following as he trotted after otter tracks on a riverbank, or even listening to his stories, I didn't know that Chris felt this way, that he would explain his own nature connection in a way that would resonate perfectly with my own reality. I just knew that being around him was to feel that I was at home in the world.

Nature connection is *my* reality check. To remember and thank coyote and the other four-leggeds (and eight-leggeds) is my reality check. But so too are storytellers like Ursula LeGuin and teachers like Tom Wessels and Chris Laliberte.

When I asked Chris about an experience of deep nature connection in his life, he told a story about coming out of a depression on a semester-long NOLS (National Outdoor Leadership School) course. Picture him: eyes blazing, hands waving, breathless...

"Getting out there was a blur, and the trip was amazing, but one really standout moment came somewhere in the Wind River Mountains of Wyoming, when I climbed on my own up on top of this large outcropping of rock overlooking a high alpine lake up in the cirque of the granite peaks. I stood up there, and the wind was really kicking, so I could lean forward against it, almost like I was flying. The sun was glinting off the waters of the lake, and the way the wind was whipping around created these amazing dancing lights on the surface of the lake that flowed like a flock of little birds, you know like starlings or something all in a cloud, at a distance where you can't really see an individual bird? The surface of the lake was rippling and flowing like that, and I just stood mesmerized. The world was truly magical, and I could SEE, and feel, the spirit in all things moving through everything in that moment. The healing power of nature, I kid you not. That was it."

III. The Elder

I brooded among a council of spruce trees on an ancient mountain peak rising from the Atlantic Ocean. I caressed the soft needles of pungent balsam fir trees in a New Hampshire riverside grove. Gazed at gnarled lodgepole pines in the gray dust of a Nevada mountain, and brushed my hands over the smooth powdery bark of aspens in the Colorado Rockies. The list goes on, through time and across landscapes to a certain cedar grove and a particular cedar tree in a Washington rainforest.

There are plenty of other magnificent trees in the Pacific

Northwest – stately Douglas firs, sinuous vine maples, sighing cottonwoods – but something about western redcedar invited me in immediately and made me want to stick around. Warm cinnamon-brown bark rises in vertical ridges, rough in areas like a grandfather's stubble and smooth in others like a grandmother's hand. Roots begin to reach and spread above ground, shoulders and elbows in the sunlight and wrists and fingers deep in the soil, so when I tuck in between two arms with the solid trunk at my back I feel both held and rooted. Above me, sprays of layered green scales fan out in arcing waves as graceful as swans' necks, no sharp edges. A slight breeze sets them all sashaying in a languid ballet.

I sit there to find quiet. I sit there to find stillness. I sit there to shed the static electricity of the insular human world and remember my place in the wild one. Cedar stands silent at my back. Solid and steady, sweet-smelling and earth-bound. No stories or lessons. No questions or answers, at least not in words. And yet, I understand that cedar knows things. Knows everything, it seems. Sitting there I start to get it. Sitting there I start to feel it, feel ego and self fade a little, allowing outside to seep inside. My breath a tree's exhalations. My exhalations a tree's breath.

I'm still an ecologist; I'm still an academic. I am hungry to learn more of the fascinating science of forest ecosystems. To wonder about, puzzle over, discover and experience on my own, yes, but also to keep learning from the biologists, the field researchers, the earth detectives who never stop asking *Why?* The deeper I delve, the more enchanting the ecology. Like the research on underground mycorrhizal networks physically and energetically connecting trees to other trees and plants and microorganisms in interspecies communication as unmistakable and as mysterious as the human nervous system. The more I learn, the more foolish I feel for ever treating non-human beings as inanimate objects. The more I learn, the more I want to bow down at the feet of this elder who has already stood in this spot for hundreds of years, who could remain here well over a thousand. And so I return, almost every day, to sit, to learn, to be thankful, and to wait for enlightenment.

Earth to Earth

When bigleaf maple leaves larger than my face turn yellow with bronze fungal spots, it is time. When the quiet, lackadaisical songbirds of late summer join in fervent, chittering mixed-species flocks, trembling the cedars, it is time. When the rains return for real and the forests won't dry until next summer, when licorice ferns green and unfurl and mushrooms of muted reds and purples appear out of dead wood overnight, it is time.

They are coming home to die.

I come to the river to watch. A silver streak in the pebbled shallows, a crimson flash that seems a trick of the eye, or the water. But no – a fin there. A whitewater tail swish, just there. Chinook, or King, salmon returning from the Pacific Ocean to spawn.

One September morning I stood not on a riverbank, but next to a rectangular holding tank containing a writhing swarm of Clackamas River Chinook. I pulled oversized rain gear and galoshes over my polyester park ranger uniform and awaited instructions from the Oregon Department of Fish and Wildlife hatchery technicians I'd volunteered to assist.

You want me to do what?

I reached in to the steel box of river water and slid a hand along a smooth, spotted coppery-red body longer than my arm, then squinted as his tail lashed water at my face. A deep white gash adorned his side like a medal, reminding me that he was one of only two or three of his parents' three thousand or more eggs that had survived not just to adulthood, he survived the journey a thousand miles and six years in the open ocean, then back up three rivers home again. *Oh, the places you've been.*

I grabbed tight, with both hands. One around his thrashing tail, the other straining to grip the thick slippery belly just behind the pectoral fins. Pulled the gasping King from the water and struggled to hold him still as he writhed. He whipped his head and tail into a rigid bow and just as quickly snapped back the other direction. Fearing I would drop him, I kneeled and bear-hugged that fifty-pound sea creature to my chest.

When I'd gained control, I stood and held the fish out away from me, placed his nose in a notched pedestal, and held on. One of the technicians raised a metal baseball bat and brought it down, thunk, on his head. The salmon went limp.

They come home to die.

Not this death, I knew, but the still rapid and no less violent death that comes from a journey so arduous it literally takes the life out of a body no longer acclimatized to fresh water, a body physically beaten, starving, and which, if it hasn't already become prey, always dies within days after spawning. Because that is the natural cycle. Life begets life.

I told myself this as I smiled and joked with the hatchery technicians and tried to pretend my hands weren't shaking. At the end of the day after I'd showered but still stank, when I still shook,

I realized they weren't the tremors of discomfort from helping kill fish.

I was giddy.

I was electrified by my intimacy with the mighty Chinook in that moment when life becomes death. An intimacy that no books, experts, or naturalist training could ever teach me. An intimacy that passive nature awareness and acute observation skills could not show me. The intimacy of death, like sex, is to know another in the deepest, most visceral sense. Hunters know this. Murderers too, I imagine.

Many of the fish I helped kill that day at the hatchery had their eggs or sperm harvested to make more hatchery salmon, then they went on to feed people. Others were trucked back to the open river and left to rot, to feed everything else. Though we may be greedy animals who take more than our share, we are learning, or maybe, remembering. Remembering that no lives are lived in isolation. That some lives reach farther than others, and continue to ripple outward even in death.

Salmon who fight their way home do more than just pass on their DNA. Salmon carcasses, whether digested by other animals or decomposed into rivers, bring ocean nutrients like nitrogen, carbon, sulfur and phosphorous that fertilize riverside plants and feed insect larvae. They in turn support entire river ecosystems, including juvenile salmon. All of which nourish forests far from rivers, down to mushrooms on cedars thick with insectivorous songbirds. Death begets life.

Mary Oliver asks us, in "The Summer Day": *What is it you plan to do with your one wild and precious life?* I ask, on a fall day, what might we do after that?

If I could, I would not seal myself in a box, nor burn my body to ashes and dust. If I could, I would give my self to the river, to be torn apart by eagles and bears, to be nibbled by fingerlings.

Soaked up by cedars or washed out to sea. To discover a new slant on intimacy.

I am not alone in this. "Green" burials are becoming more common in the West, and for more than just environmental reasons. Instead of chemical embalming and hermetically sealed steel boxes, shrouds and cardboard. Instead of urns interred in marble mausoleums, ashes thrown to the wind or waves. Or planted with seeds to grow into trees. I would prefer to feed a cougar or a murder of crows, but barring such luck, planted with a cedar sapling in a Pacific Northwest riverside forest would do.

But I'm not just talking about my body. We all more or less accept the idea that our physical bodies stick around here, dust to dust. Whether we attempt to seal ourselves from the earth or not, the earth will eventually take us back. But what about the invisible parts, our life forces, vital energy, or yes, souls that might pass on?

We naturally wonder more about this as we grow older, as we watch loved ones die. Old age, accidents, cancer. Suicides. When someone wants more than anything else to be gone from here, where do they go?

What if an afterlife exists, but, as multiple religions seem to suggest, somewhere else, up in the proverbial sky or in some other dimension? Maybe somewhere with other human souls but without the warmth of our sun, the ocean breeze or rain-soaked earth, somewhere without trees, rivers, birds, bugs, or salmon?

No matter how pleasant it might be, no matter how blissfully serene, I don't want to go there. Earth is the place I want to stay. Whether that means I come back as another awkward and struggling human or a battered and struggling Chinook is no matter. As long as I come back. When I die, I don't want to leave. I want to come home.

It's fall again; time to return to the river. I came in hopes of spying that silver flash I can still feel in my hands, against my body. I'm looking for life, but finding none, I follow a familiar smell to the source. There, in the shade of a yellowing cottonwood on river-smoothed stones. Eyes already pecked out, dulled white teeth in a broken jaw, battle scars on a sleek body longer than my arm. Nearby, a raven watches.

Niche

Panic flickered in my eyes, wild and darting up and down, back and forth in the shadows. *Do you need to move closer to the door?* someone said. *Yes please*, I whispered, and crawled over legs and feet, brushed elbows and hands, accidentally stepped on someone's long braid and bumped my head on a protruding knot in the willow branch frame of the sweat lodge that seemed to be closing in on me and the twenty-six other people filling every space like an overfull lifeboat. I wheedled into a spot in the outer ring of strangers huddled around the center pile of fire-heated rocks. I pressed my backbone into the branch that curved over and above me, tried not to think about the layers of heavy blankets enclosing the frame, the thick black plastic above that. I reached behind me, followed the branch down to the blanket floor and jabbed and burrowed fingers under it to find the earth's coolness. I clawed dirt under my fingernails, clenched gravel in my fist. We hadn't even started yet.

I was breathing too fast, using up too much air, which seemed deficient in here as it was. I trained my eyes on the three-square-foot opening to the outside. Out there a hemlock, cedar, and fir swayed freely in the open air against a gray sky, tossing raindrops in the cool September morning. I wanted to be out there. Why was I in here?

Our leader ladled water over the scorched rocks in the center and they hissed humidity into my face. All remaining fresh air transformed into stifling steam. Then someone pulled the outer plastic and inner blanket doors to the earth, sealing us in darkness.

I heard some of the other participants breathing deeply but none seemed to be panting as I was. I already forgot who sat nearest me but the one to my left shifted a sweaty elbow into my ribs. When I flinched and recoiled to the right, hair brushed my shoulder. I pulled my knees to my chest and dropped my head to meet them.

Four to five hours we were going to be in that lodge, sweating in the darkness. I wasn't going to make it.

Why was I freaking out? Didn't we all come from dark, warm, enclosed spaces? From thick breathable fluid in which we grew and stretched our walls around us. Tethered in place by a single lifeline, like astronauts, until finally we squeezed our way out. Or we were pulled from below or snatched from above. Why do I find that terrifying?

How do we not?

~

You build your lodge in a pond or slow-moving river for protection. Though you are adapted for life in and around the water, you are a land mammal. You need to breathe air, can only hold your breath for fifteen minutes at the most. Your food, the inner bark of willow, cottonwood, alder and other trees, grows on solid earth, not water. Yet home is a watery cave.

After excavating a depression at the water's bottom, you layer branches and sticks, mud and sod into a rounded structure like an earthen igloo. A door several feet underwater tunnels up to an inner chamber above the water level. That one room might house your mate, up to five yearlings and up to five younger kits. You'll all spend the winter here, wide awake in the darkness. In northern regions where the water freezes, you will be trapped within it. The only fresh air a tiny vent in the roof of your lodge. Your only food what you've collected in the frigid, deep-water cache outside your door.

You chose this life, or your ancestors did, because it's safer than what's outside – animals swifter and more cunning than you. Bobcat and river otter. Red fox and coyote. Human. All the dangers of the open water and earth. Lodges are strong, warm, and safe. They house a family. They are home. You aren't afraid of the dark. Danger walks in the light.

~

I drove into Boulder, Colorado, from the north, my station wagon full of my belongings. Naked yellow foothills loomed on my right. To my left brown prairie stretched on into eternity. I'd driven though Colorado before, had visited similar landscapes of open rangeland, high desert, and grasslands on my journeys between the more lush, forested eastern landscapes of my youth and West Coast forays of my adulthood. But that day, I was moving there. Newly single, starting over. That day, the landscape felt different.

I pulled into a wildlife viewing area parking lot facing the prairie, got out and tried to take it all in. I leaned against my car and breathed the late October air, dusty and stagnant. Faded grasses and bronzed rabbitbrush huddled, still, and grey splintered fences extended to the horizon. The temperature was comfortable but I could see how parched the earth was, imagined the tumbleweeds blowing in the scorching summer windstorms. At almost 6,000 feet I knew, too, that I was in for a harsh winter with heavy blowing snows and bitter cold.

As a naturalist I knew it was a rich landscape that at times hosted myriad wildflowers and woody shrubs, birds and reptiles, insects and bats. Right then, it just looked empty. The two words that came to mind in that landscape, that will forever come to my mind in such landscapes to make me shudder and sigh, are *exposed* and *barren*.

The earth was flat, stretching away from me, and I was stretched with it. I was exposed. I was barren. I just might have dried up and blown away on the prairie wind, but for the weight in my chest. I got back in my car and shut the door.

~

Some call you antelope, because of your similarity to the Old World, hoofed mammal, but you are the only remaining member of an ancient family. Your closest living relative is a giraffe. Your real name is pronghorn, for the hook on your horn that is technically neither horn nor antler. But despite our inability to place you in our neat categories, you know where you fit. Only, and always, in the open.

Arid grasslands, shrub steppe, and sagebrush deserts of western North America. You avoid woodlands. You want to see forever. You almost can; your powerful vision is made stronger by eyes high and protruding from opposite sides of your skull. You can spy movement four miles away.

And if danger somehow found its way close to you? No matter, you are built for speed. By far the fastest North American land mammal, you can sustain speeds above fifty-five miles an hour, some say up to seventy miles an hour for several minutes. Only the cheetah is faster, but briefly, in bursts.

Finally, if danger were to reach you, you would use your sharp hooves to kick, stab, stomp. You would fight to the end. *See, run, fight,* you know these words well. *Hide?* That would never occur to you.

You don't even take shelter from the elements. Your body is all the shelter you need. Hollow hairs fluff out to cool you on searing hot days, and flatten against your body to seal in warmth in frigid cold. Rather than seek protection in the coldest times, you may move even higher into the hills or other exposed areas, seeking the places where wind is more likely to have blown the snow away from shrubby browse.

In the open, you are safe. You aim to always see what's coming, all the dangers that could otherwise sneak up on you unaware. Bobcat and cougar. Wolf and coyote. Human. You are home on the range, roaming day and night, without shelter or even a home bed. You aren't afraid of the light. Danger lurks in the dark.

~

I tucked into a perfectly me-sized hollow beneath stilted hemlock roots. Spongy duff of hemlock and cedar needles and a mesh of rootlets cradled me, mocha brown packed earth pressed my back, and rough roots curled down above me. I was the meat in a forest burrito. I oriented my face toward the forest, an open understory punctuated occasionally by bouquets of sword ferns, so I averted the claustrophobia that might normally follow me into a cave-like space. I breathed in the odd aridity of a Western Washington week without rain at a time of year that you can still smell it. Though my body would stay dry that day, in that almost-rainforest in spring, the memory of rain always lingers like a faint perfume.

I was hiding. Adult hide-and-seek. For the first few minutes my heart rapped and my smile threatened to give way to school-girl giggles bubbling up from my chest. But time passed with no action. Adults are sneaky, especially outdoorsy adults with wilderness scouting training, and we were patient. Our area of play was huge, and we were in no hurry. I snuggled in, let my ear drop to the soft earth and sighed.

The Pacific wren that had a few minutes earlier chipped and chirped in alarm at my scrambling, began to sing. That little brown meatball with a tail perched on a cedar stump six feet from my nose and spilled note after note of the speediest, most jumbled, yet sweetest song of Western Washington's early spring. Farther off a raven *cronk*ed her own speech into the air, answered by another.

I'd lived in the region less than a year; everyone and everything still new. And I was lying in the dirt in a dank forest. Why did I feel so at home?

I didn't want to be found. Not just to win the game; it was more than that. I didn't want to come out from the earth. I was held. Like the pressure of a hug, or more, the full contact of a lover's body on mine. No warm mammal but the cool earth. No open expression of love and care, but the pressure of the earth itself. Which, right then, was better. Easier. I was supported but not depleted. Anchored there, yet free to breathe and see out and leave when I liked. I felt perfectly comfortable and completely safe.

~

We evolved out of arid savannah, we used to believe. That is why we might prefer the open country. Then we learned that those African deserts were once moist forests. That is why we might prefer the woodlands. But every starting point is arbitrary, isn't it? On a long enough timeline our species has wandered everywhere, made our homes all along the way. Where will our bodies be most comfortable – the landscape where we were born and raised? Or that of our families, generations before us? How about our ancestors? How about their predecessors? How far might our memories stretch?

Fear, too, has deep and branching roots. Were you ever trapped in an enclosed space? Maybe a snow cave collapsed on you and you couldn't breathe, couldn't claw your way out, didn't even know which way to the light. Maybe you were locked in a closet or confined in a broken elevator. Maybe you awoke in the dark in a stranger's bed.

Or, were you ever lost in a crowd, a child in a department store or on a city street, nothing or no one familiar in sight? Do you get dizzy with no frame of reference—do you stagger and stumble? Have you ever felt in danger with no place to hide? Was someone chasing you? Hunting you? A person, your past, your loneliness...

Maybe not. Maybe in reality you've always been safe, inside or out. And maybe you're scared anyway. Perhaps our memories stretch back farther, before our bodies came along. Genetic, innate, what the scientists call "prepared phobias." Lions are out there – don't be seen! The big bad wolf will find you – don't get cornered! Every starting point is arbitrary. Our past, our family's, our ancestors', their predecessors'... what of our animal cousins?

~

You evolved out of arid savannah, we believe. When my ancestors first met you on this continent, they called you *prairie wolf*, to differentiate you from your larger, more feared cousin, the timber wolf. And though we did our best to extirpate you along with all the larger predators we still fear, you have only flourished. Our imagined enemies were your real ones, and you took advantage of the lions', bears', and wolves' absences to move into their territories. You took advantage of our agricultural fields for browsing crops and hunting small mammals. Clear-cuts for the same. Even suburban towns and cities offer up bounty, of human food, pet food, human pets, and the rats who will outlive us all. You adapted to all of it, even to us. We've poisoned you, shot your children, trapped and skinned your elders, yet whenever your population dips, you relax your social hierarchy and breed more, raise more pups, replenishing your numbers. You are a survivor.

Now, you roam throughout North America, in every habitat type. Your omnivorous diet, social structures, and behaviors vary based on the landscapes where you make your home. You prefer some combination of open country and protected cover where you can be hunter or hidden, as need be. You typically make your home an open-ended, tunnel-like den in a hillside, streambank, brush pile, hollow log, or dug under the root wad of a large downed tree.

~

I sat on a pile of leaves and conifer needles in the space between where two large roots of a western redcedar tree sloped to the ground. Back against the thick bark and elbows resting on the roots, I surveyed the forest in front of me. It was December in Western Washington, dry and cold for a few days between rains. I pulled my fleece hat down to cover my ears and tucked my hands into the opposite arms of my wool jacket.

I breathed in the cold and the quiet. The Douglas squirrel who lived in the Douglas fir stump across the open cedar grove was nowhere to be seen, though he no longer bothered to squeak and chatter at me after seeing me there regularly. The black-tailed deer who fed in the nearby meadow at dawn and dusk might have been nestled somewhere nearby, as their heart-shaped tracks paralleled mine in our habitual routes, but I couldn't see them, nor any other living mammal. The birds, too, were silent on that day; the green conifers and naked brown maples and cottonwoods were still.

By most definitions, I was alone. Yet the cedar tree was strong at my back, under my arms. Dried maple leaves insulated me from the cold earth. Emerald sword ferns, Oregon grape leaves, and lush mosses softened the winter browns, and in the spaces between the deciduous trees in the distance I could see the open river valley and white-capped Cascades mountains. Three thousand miles from my birthplace, no family member nor human friend within shouting distance or even a short drive, yet I knew I had found my true home. I was safe.

And then, gunshots rang out. Loud! I cringed and gripped the tree, looked around wildly for the source, though I knew by then that the shooter was probably down in the valley, a half mile from there. Probably shooting waterfowl, or just targets. A normal part of living in the country, out West. I would eventually get used to it, they said. Maybe. But right then my heart was beating too fast. Right then I was panting. I pulled my knees to my chest and dropped my head.

A few minutes later, leaves rustled across the cedar grove. A furred mammal leapt over the hillside that sloped up from the streambank. Pointed ears and snout with a moist black nose, chestnut-brown and grey fur with a bushy black-tipped tail.

She froze, one paw in the air.

I froze, still clenching my cedar tree.

And then, I exhaled. Still holding her gaze, I let my shoulders drop away from my ears. Loosened my grip on the tree and lowered my legs back to the forest floor. My head dropped back against the bark. I breathed easy.

Coyote put her paw down. Took a few slow steps on a line parallel with me, looked behind her, then back at me. Then, sat down.

She looked at me, blinked.

I looked at her, smiled and breathed.

She blinked again, cocked her head, and trotted away. I stayed.

Blood & Ink

My first time, I was nineteen, with my eighteen-year-old boyfriend, Michael. I don't remember whose idea it was, only that we had both wanted it for as long as we could remember. My parents thought he was a bad influence on me; his parents thought I was the bad seed. They were probably both right. But though we felt a little thrill at what we were doing behind their backs, we knew we were doing nothing wrong.

Because I attended college in quaint, well-behaved Charlottesville, Virginia, and he in inner city Washington, D.C., it made sense to do it in his neighborhood. We found the place in the yellow pages. We were smart enough to do a little research, to make sure the shop had some sort of licensing, that it looked clean. We didn't want diseases; we just wanted tattoos.

Clean, yes. But also dark, and ear-splittingly loud with heavy-metal guitar and drums, and bikers hanging out in the front room. Real bikers – black bandanas, leather jackets and steel-toed boots. Harleys parked outside. It was the antithesis of our suburban Connecticut hometown. Perfect.

Michael went first. The grizzled and aging tattoo artist, skin leather-tanned and inked on all visible surfaces except hands and face, revved up his tattoo gun. Like a hand-held sewing machine, except instead of needling thread into fabric, it needles ink into epidermis and screams like a dentist's drill. He started working on one arm while I held on to Michael's other. Head bowed, shaggy dark hair falling over moody wolfish eyes, Michael muttered *Fuck, that fucking hurts* and gripped my hand so hard it turned white.

Ink soon mixed with blood dribbling down his bicep. The artist alternately drilled and swiped a paper towel across the red and black smears. Drill. Wipe. *Ow, fuck.*

I didn't swear when it was my turn in the chair. I didn't say anything at all until the tattoo artist looked up at my face and asked, *Are you okay?* Tears streamed down my cheeks, dripped onto my chest and mixed with the blood and ink over my heart. It did fucking hurt. But I was okay.

Later that night I lay with Michael in his single bed in the George Washington University freshman dorm, hyper-aware and protective of our respective bandaged wounds. Unlike most nights in our two years together, we didn't have sex. We lay there, holding hands in that exhausted exhilarated post-adrenalated state. He, marked with a skull and crossbones inside a black spade—the death card. I, marked with a red rose dripping with morning dew—my tribute to love and life. Indelible ink that made our bodies more definitively our own than they had been before.

They said I'd regret it. They said, *What if you change your mind?* They said I would be judged, wouldn't be able to get jobs, would burn in hell. *They* will always point fingers and condemn differences. For those of us who feel we *are* different, a little awkward, a little too loud or quiet or angry or confused, those of us who don't want the things we're supposed to want or have never easily fit in even when trying, marking ourselves is one way of owning it. Maybe I'm not like everyone else. Fine.

But yes, I did regret that first one. I'll own that too.

The design was not an original drawing, but a generic picture chosen from stock drawings tacked to the wall of the shop. "Flash," they're called. The rose over my heart quite possibly adorned some other girl's chest or hip. Some girl like Michael's next girlfriend, for whom he dumped me. After my second failed relationship by the age of twenty and a family history of more failed marriages and messy divorces than a Hollywood gossip column, I was starting to believe that maybe romantic love wasn't the meaning of life. Not mine anyway.

So, in a quiet studio back in suburban Connecticut, a bookish art major with a neat ponytail started to needle purple and blue over the red and green. While I sucked on peppermints and listened to ambient gypsy electronica, the dewy rose disappeared, metamorphosed into a dragonfly rising from the water. One blue droplet is all that remains from my first time.

Though by no means rare in the tattoo world, this was *my* dragonfly. The artist drew it for me, based on field guide photographs and my own description of what I wanted. Nobody accompanied me. I held my own hand.

Dragonflies begin their lives in water as dull brown naiads, then climb onto land, break out of their old shells, inflate iridescent wings and fly. Beautiful, delicate little fairies, yet agile, deadly hunters of insects. Mosquito hawks. Dragon flies. But these weren't the only reasons for my new ink.

I was wandering in the woods one day, alone as I increasingly preferred to be, when I came to an open wetland meadow. The trail there turned to boardwalk, and I chose a spot warmed by early spring sun to pause and bask by a rippling pool. When a thrumming sound drew my eye to the water, I saw a dragonfly there, struggling in the surface tension. Drowning. Though I didn't understand right away why a dragonfly would be unable to lift from the water and fly, I nevertheless put belly to boardwalk, paddled water toward me so the dragon would float my way, and when I could reach him scooped him up in my hand. One wing looked a little crooked, but otherwise he seemed whole and undamaged. I sat back on the boardwalk and placed him gently on my knee. Six black legs clasped my blue jeans. I leaned back, knees up and palms down behind me. He held on in the breeze, wings flexing occasionally.

After an hour, when his new wings were dry and fully inflated, he lifted off. Instead of the emptiness of love lost, what I felt was the fullness of a different kind of connection.

The dragonfly on my chest is that dragonfly. My dragonfly. The day it became part of me, it was as if I climbed out of my old skin and grew wings.

More wings followed, a black-inked raven on my left foot. A ring of bats around my right ankle. Then a woman chasing a flaming sun on my shoulder blade and an oak tree on my left forearm. Each new tattoo a symbolic image with a personal story of connection. A story I want to remember. My body becoming a field guide of its own, a field guide to me.

Marking the body with dyes is as old as art, with evidence found in multiple cultures on every continent. Tattoos as healing acupuncture dots or ash rubbed in wounds, tattoos as rites of passage or hennaed wedding decorations. Plant dyes mixed with animal fat as warrior markings for strength and prestige. Sailors' identification, in case of being lost at sea.

As Western civilization became more "civilized" (more *they* to point fingers at *not-them*), tattoos were relegated to outsiders. Pagans, barbarians, slaves, pirates, lower class. Bikers, punks, gang members, and other rebels. So I understand why the idea of tattoos makes those in charge nervous. But when a part-time job pouring ice water and supplying clean towels in an upscale healing-arts spa told me I had to wear an ace bandage over the tree on my arm so as not to offend their clientele, I quit after one day. When my state park employer told me their dress code required me to wear long sleeves over that tree year-round, despite the fact that I was hired as a naturalist to teach people about trees, I ignored it. Thankfully I had an open-minded supervisor willing to ignore me ignoring it.

Am I a nonconformist? Not usually, no. I like structure and appreciate rules when they make sense to me. I'm more likely to be called anal-retentive or goody-two-shoes than rebel. Always on time, almost always doing what's expected of me. But rules that prohibit me from marking my own body with pictures of birds and bugs and trees, images that wouldn't possibly offend if worn on clothing? That's just bigotry. That's prejudice. People who judge me as lesser for having art on my body, or who cater to those who would, are not people I want to work for or befriend. The more art I wear, the easier it is for me to weed those people out of my life.

Fine, maybe I am a nonconformist.

And yes, in some ways, a masochist. I don't enjoy the pain itself, and unlike reactive self-harm such as punching walls or cutting, I can't just walk into a tattoo studio when anxious or furious and get that release on demand. Not a respectable tattoo studio anyway. Getting a custom tattoo often takes multiple consultation appointments or at least a few weeks' or months' wait for skilled artists, not to mention hundreds of dollars (though they do tend to take credit cards). But the pain has a way of refocusing whatever feelings happen to be there at the time, transforming or even healing buried wounds.

In a backyard tattoo studio in Portland, Oregon, sunshiny and painted in reds and oranges, I sat backwards straddling a chair, hugging a pillow to my naked chest while a lithe, heron-like woman tattooed a Pacific willow across my back from shoulders to tailbone. In two separate sittings of two-and-a-half hours each, I shook and cried as she shaped leaves and carved bark, pausing to wipe away blood and spray a cooling anesthetic.

For my seventh tattoo, on this meaty, muscular part of my body, the intense pain took me by surprise. I hadn't cried since the first, and this time I was bawling. More than ever before I felt as if the tattoo gun drilled directly into raw nerves, splitting me open, shredding my very core. It was no coincidence that I was in the midst of the most painful breakup of my life to that point, a long-term committed relationship with a woman I would have married had that been legal at the time. We had life plans, a future together. Until we didn't. Until the day I found the strength to pack up my things and drive away from her deceits and my clingy desperation.

I was broken, damaged and raging beyond taking deep breaths and counting to ten. Beyond meditating and even beyond taking a long quiet walk in the woods. I needed to claw my way out of my old skin once again, to start over new. I needed pain; I needed blood. Judge me if you want, but I'm talking about my own body. My own catharsis. About marking myself with beauty instead of ugliness. In that backyard studio, the cool steady hands of the heron woman ripped me apart and remade me with a strong trunk and full leafy crown. A flexible tree with deep roots that bends in the wind and doesn't break.

That willow tree, like the oak on my arm, is thought to have powerful magic symbolism not only to my pagan, Celtic ancestors, but to my own increasingly nature-centered pagan spirituality. Mine is a quiet, personal spirituality I rarely speak of and usually only experience alone, outside. But it has to do with the stuff of all religions, of finding deep meaning beyond our small human lives, of connecting to a benevolent force greater than all of us. A force I've glimpsed in all manner of flora and fauna, whether a newly hatched dragonfly or a willow tree in a sun-dappled grove. It's a force recognized by peoples everywhere, regardless of official practices or religions. Tattoo number eight, the Celtic knotted snake on my right arm, and nine, the Pacific Northwest salmon on my right thigh, were homage not just to individual creatures but to earth cultures, the peoples of my past and present homes.

I forget what number I'm on now, but I remember all the stories. The barred owl in the cedar forest, cougar tracks in the snow, the Anna's hummingbird alighting on my hand, and the silvery blue butterfly I watched for hours while sitting in the sun by the Columbia River, until a bird swooped in and ate him in one mouthful. Memories and reminders of what's most real. What matters to me. The calypso orchids of moist, montane forests, the orb weavers at my windows, and a black widow in the skylight of a cob house in the Californian desert. Beauty and nurturing, the places I've been healed. These images on my body are my spiritual teachers, my gurus, my gods. My tattoos are my field guide, but also my bible, my sutra.

It was time. I headed in to Portland's New Rose Tattoo for an appointment with Mikal. A punky artist with spiked hair and an easy smile, he beckoned me through the swinging doors with the winged heart to his booth, where I reclined under a warrior mask and a bighorn sheep skull while he mixed ink. With the first stings of the needle I gripped the black vinyl chair until my hand turned white, but I remained quiet, remembered to breathe.

With needles, ink and blood Mikal cast a new spell on my body. A picture spell, like a pictograph, that will last as long as my body does. This new tattoo was magic in itself. More wings, another bird, but this one? A phoenix. I have not yet had enough of being reborn.

Borderline

It comes on the wind, with September. The edginess that stretches you thin. Birds flit faster, frantic. Trains shrill louder; sirens scream past; city coyotes go crazy, keening. You understand. Even when you're sitting still, your mind paces.

You have to get out of here.

It is time to leave home, move back to the wilderness, quit your job, lose your mind, something, anything, but it's time. So you go. Get in your car, and drive. Find a place that makes sense right now, a place more restless, more mixed up than you.

East or west? The Pacific Ocean edge of the continent, the salted mist shroud over white-noise waves? Not today. Today, the wind carries you east, to a different precipice.

Follow the train tracks along the Columbia River and watch the fresh fertile greens of moss-adorned maple, cedar, and fern fade to rusty yellows and browns of scrubby white oak, red-barked ponderosa pine, and drying hay fields. Drive until the naked reds and blacks of ancient lava flows loom above, and leave the flood-carved river bottom for higher ground. From *fire danger low* to *fire danger extreme* in two hours. Find yourself, then, on Rowena Plateau, in Tom McCall Preserve, and know that you are exactly where you need to be.

This is the transition zone. Where the last of the coastal moisture is wrung out against the Cascade Range, but not yet the high desert and bunchgrass prairie of the parched east side. The place in between. Where the azure Columbia runs below to the north and white-capped Mt. Hood rises above to the south. The place in between. Where Burlington Northern Santa Fe engines haul coal, where tractor trailers and passenger cars zoom along the interstate to and from civilization, but where no human dwells. The place in between. Arid East or waterlogged West, river valley or mountain peak, city or wilderness; what is this place? Both. Neither. Yes.

On the precipice, the wind is fierce. Wander the cliffs until you find the place where the cool air takes the edge off the late summer sun but won't make you shiver with impending autumn. Then sit on a lichen-blackened rock and fade into the landscape.

What is wind? A clash of temperatures, of pressures. Wind is edginess incarnate. Watch how it impels the dried grasses blanketing the plateau. Amber waves of grain? No, not liquid waves but erratic quaking, trembling, tremors. Like time-elapse photography, faster even than the thoughts in your brain. So fast you can be still.

Listen. Behind the drone of trains and traffic is the buzzing and clicking of grasshoppers, like castanets, popping up out of nowhere and then disappearing again into the terra cotta dust. Somewhere nearby rise tentative twitters of juncos and goldfinches, shadows of their bold westside selves. The wind speaks too, whistling to the stunted oaks, shushing the grasses, and crackling the papery leaves of April's balsamroot flowers.

Behind the wind is quiet. You can hear that too, if you try. This landscape is large enough to swallow noise and spit out silence. See the turkey vultures above, climbing, circling, rocking back and forth. Focus out and they are still, hanging in the sky, frozen.

Pumpkin-colored butterflies dart around, seeking the few remaining bits of color in this washed-out landscape—sky-blue bachelor buttons and ballet-pink wooly pussytoes. Ever in motion, too fast to see, until one lands on your shoe, stops. Fuzzy white body, yellow-green eyes, splotched brown wings closed tight. You hold your breath, stay still, stretch time until the inevitable. Butterfly jolts to life and is gone.

You've read that there are more than two hundred plant species here, and several only found in the Columbia Gorge, like Columbia desert parsley and Thompson's broadleaf lupine. Edges nurture diversity. You know that the spring wildflower show is spectacular, have braved the crowds of photographers and naturalists for glimpses of purple grass widows and pink prairie stars.

But September is the end of abundance, the pendulum swing toward winter, when the brightest color is huge swaths of reddening poison oak encircling two cattail ponds sunk into the lava rock. Wetland islands that in spring host singing frogs and redwing blackbirds, inches from scrubby desert shrubs. Contradiction? Paradox? Here, it somehow all fits.

You can be anything here. Or nothing; it doesn't matter. The wind doesn't care. The rock doesn't care. The Steller's jay calling in the swaying ponderosa might care a little. Why is he so worked up, anyway? You can't see any reason to worry, about anything. You've forgotten. What were the questions, again?

Do you belong to the city or the wilds? Are you human or animal? Are you sane or lunatic?

Both? Neither? Yes.

End Notes

Bite Marks
Nagasawa, Miho, et al. "Oxytocin-gaze positive loop and the coevolution of human-dog bonds." *Science* Vol. 348 no. 6232 (2015): 333-336. Print.

Hand Wing
Bat Conservation International. "Bats Are Important." Web. Accessed 29 July 2018. www.batcon.org/why-bats/bats-are-important.

Catch and Release
Kellerman, J., Lewis, J., & Laird, J.D.. "Looking and loving: The effects of mutual gaze on feelings of romantic love." *Journal of Research in Personality*. Volume 23, issue 2 (1989): 145-161. Print.

C Is for Cat
Dillard, Annie. "Living Like Weasels." *Teaching a Stone to Talk*. New York: HarperCollins Publishers, 1982. p. 29. Print.

Paradise Prison
Kerouac, Jack. *Desolation Angels.* New York: Riverhead Books, 1965. p. 3. Print.

Fast Freight
The Kingston Trio. "Fast Freight." *The Kingston Trio,* Capitol Records, 1958.

The Road Well-Traveled
The Eagles. "Life in the Fast Lane." *Hotel California*, Asylum, 1976.
Steve Miller Band. "Fly Like an Eagle." *Fly Like an Eagle*, Capitol Records, 1976.

Destiny Manifested
Snyder, Gary. *A Place in Space*. Washington, D.C.: Counterpoint, 1995. p. 43. Print.

Speaking Bird
U.S. Fish & Wildlife Service. "Economic Impact: Birds, Bird Watching and the U.S. Economy." Web. Accessed 29 July, 2018. www.fws.gov/birds/bird-enthusiasts/bird-watching/valuing-birds.php.

Bodhi Tree
Wessels, Tom. *Reading the Forested Landscape*. Woodstock, VT: The Countryman Press, 1997. p. 15. Print.
Le Guin, Ursula. "Buffalo Gals Won't You Come Out Tonight." *Buffalo Gals and Other Animal Presences*. New York, NY: Penguin Books, 1987. 17-60. Print.

Earth to Earth
Oliver, Mary. "The Summer Day." *House of Light*. Boston, MA: Beacon Press, 1990. p. 60. Print.

Acknowledgments

I am grateful to the editors of the following publications in which earlier drafts of these essays first appeared: "Hand Wing" in *Tahoma Literary Review,* "Feral" in *Soundings Review,* "Prey" in *Animal Literary Magazine,* "Destiny Manifested" in *Cirque Literary Journal,* "Earth to Earth" in *Blue Lyra Review,* and "Blood and Ink" in *Bacopa Literary Review.*

I am deeply indebted to Ana Maria Spagna and Larry Cheek for helping me learn how to craft my insular musings into essays that might appeal to other humans, and for other mentors who added their unique voices along the way, especially Kathleen Dean Moore, Kim Stafford, and David Oates. I am also grateful to fellow MFA nonfiction classmates who provided valuable feedback and encouragement, and the whole NILA community who have been and continue to be more supportive than I could have hoped. To publisher Jill McCabe Johnson and editor Julie Riddle with Trail to Table Press for believing in my work, for treating it tenderly, and for letting me remain true to my vision. And to my family for being exactly who they are, and letting me be me.

I am thankful for all the scientists, storytellers, and nature writers who started me on this path, and even more thankful for those without words who picked up where they left off. For the birds, especially goshawk, owl, raven, hummingbird, dipper, and wren. For the four-leggeds, especially cat, bobcat, cougar, deer, and coyote. For bats and snakes and frogs and spiders – I got your back. Plants and trees, especially cottonwood, cedar, hemlock, and fir. Rivers, rain, oceans, and salmon. Granite and sandstone, sunshine, and Mother Earth herself. Thank you for our home.

CPSIA information can be obtained
at www.ICGtesting.com
Printed in the USA
LVHW082356010419
612627LV00007B/246/P